1-2-3 Magic

Effective Discipline for Children 2-12

Fourth Edition

1-2-3 Magic

Fourth Edition

Thomas W. Phelan, Ph.D.

ParentMagic, Inc.
Glen Ellyn, Illinois

Illustrations by Dan Farrell
Graphic Design by Mary Navolio
Distributed by Independent Publishers Group

Printed in the United States of America
10 9 8 7 6

For more information, contact:
ParentMagic, Inc.
800 Roosevelt Road
Glen Ellyn, Illinois 60137

Publisher's Cataloging-in-Publication
(Provided by Quality Books, Inc.)

Phelan, Thomas W., 1943-
  1-2-3 magic / Thomas W. Phelan. -- 4th ed.
  p. cm.
  Includes bibliographical references and index.
  ISBN-13: 978-1-889140-43-8
  ISBN-10: 1-889140-43-0

  1. Discipline of children. 2. Parenting.
I. Title.

HQ770.4.P44 2010   649'.64
                              QBI10-2175

to Eileen

Contents

PART IV: ENCOURAGING GOOD BEHAVIOR (Job #2)

PART V: STRENGTHENING YOUR RELATIONSHIP WITH YOUR CHILDREN (Job #3)

PART VI: ENJOYING YOUR NEW FAMILY LIFE

Preface to the
4th Edition of *1-2-3 Magic*

1-2-3 *Magic* is a simple, precise and effective way of managing—gently and firmly—the behavior of children in approximately the two-to-twelve-year-old age range. It is not magic. The reason for our unusual title is that so many parents, teachers and other child caretakers have said, "It works like magic!" *1-2-3 Magic* certainly does work if you do it correctly, which means following a few basic rules. The 1-2-3 is what you might call a "parents-in-charge" strategy, but no arguing, yelling or spanking is allowed. Raising kids is *unexpectedly hard*, and it really, really helps to know what you're doing.

If you are raising young children, *1-2-3 Magic* might be your ticket to effective and enjoyable parenting for several reasons:

1. The book has sold over *1,250,000 copies*.

2. *1-2-3 Magic* has been translated into *20 languages*.

3. Over the last several years, the 3rd Edition has consistently been the *#1 child discipline book* on Amazon.com.

4. The program is *dad-friendly*.

5. It's evidence-based—that means *it works*.

For Best Results

This Fourth Edition of *1-2-3 Magic* describes straightforward methods for managing the behavior of children from the ages of approximately two to twelve, whether they're average or special needs kids. You can actually start at about 18 months with a typically developing youngster. To get the best results, keep in mind the following:

1. The strategies should be used exactly as they are described here, especially with regard to the No-Talking and No-Emotion Rules.

2. If both parents are living at home, ideally both adults should use the program. If one parent refuses to use *1-2-3 Magic*, however, the other parent can still use it on his or her own (while hoping, of course, that their partner or spouse is doing something reasonable with the kids).

Quik Tip
If you are parenting on your own, you are very likely to feel overloaded, and you don't have a lot of time to spend learning discipline programs. Also because you're by yourself, you cannot afford to be inefficient when it comes to managing your children. You only have so much energy!

3. Single, separated and divorced parents can use our methods effectively by themselves. It is preferable if all parents—even if they are in different locations—are using the same program, but that isn't always possible. In fact, single parents greatly benefit from a simple and effective system like the "1-2-3." If you are parenting on your own, you are very likely to feel overloaded, and you don't have a lot of time to spend learning discipline programs. Also, because you're by yourself, you cannot afford to be inefficient when it comes to managing your children. You only have so much energy!

4. Grandparents, babysitters and other caregivers have also found the 1-2-3 very helpful in managing young children. Actually, many grandparents first discovered *1-2-3 Magic* on their own and then shared it with their children. In addition, we hear more and more these days that grandparents are raising their grandchildren themselves, and these adults often find *1-2-3 Magic* to be a lifesaver.

5. Make sure your kids are in good physical health. It is a well-known fact that illness, allergies and physical pain can aggravate both

behavioral and emotional problems in children. Regular physical exams for the kids are of critical importance. It's also important to know and respect your children's natural daily rhythms regarding food, sleep and bathroom. A child who missed a nap, who feels hungry or who has to go to the bathroom can be much more challenging.

Psychological Evaluation and Counseling

When in the process of using *1-2-3 Magic,* is it necessary to get a mental health professional involved?

Psychological evaluation and counseling are indicated *before* using *1-2-3 Magic* if any child has a history of excessive separation anxiety, physical violence or extremely self-punitive behavior. These children can be very difficult to manage during the initial testing period when they are still adjusting to the new discipline.

If your family is *currently* in counseling, this program should be discussed with the counselor before you use it. If your counselor is not familiar with *1-2-3 Magic*, take a copy of the book, DVD or audio CD for him or her to become familiar with.

Psychological evaluation and counseling are indicated *after* using *1-2-3 Magic* if:

1. Marital instability or conflict are interfering with the effective use of the methods. *1-2-3 Magic* is normally an excellent way to get Mom and Dad "on the same page" in dealing with the kids. Sometimes just a few counseling sessions can help right the ship.

2. One or both parents are incapable of following the No-Talking and No-Emotion Rules (see Chapter 3). Life stressors, as well as problems such as anxiety and depression, can make it hard for some parents to calm down enough to effectively use *1-2-3 Magic*. Drug and alcohol use can also make moms and dads volatile, obnoxious and ineffective.

3. Behavior problems, as well as testing and manipulation by the child, are continuing at too high a level for more than three weeks after starting the program. Your child was hard to manage before *1-2-3 Magic*. Now he's better, but you still feel managing him is too much of a grind. Check it out with a professional.

4. Trust your instincts. Here's a good rule of thumb: If you have been worrying about a particular problem in your child *for more than six months*, that's too long. See a mental health professional and find out if there is, in fact, something wrong. If there is, try to fix it or learn how to manage it. If there's nothing wrong, stop worrying.

Serious psychological and behavioral problems in young children frequently include persistent difficulties with the following:

- Paying attention or sitting still
- Language development, social interaction, and restricted interests
- Negative, hostile and defiant behavior
- Excessive worrying or unusual anxiety about separation
- Loss of interest in fun activities and irritability
- Excessive verbal and physical aggression
- Disregard for age-appropriate norms and rules
- Unexpected learning difficulties

What's New in the Fourth Edition?

The Fourth Edition of *1-2-3 Magic* has many changes. These changes reflect our own opinions about what should be different, but they also include over three dozen ideas that came from our readers, viewers, listeners and other clients. The changes include:

1. A new, more thorough, easier-to-use Index

2. A new Appendix for further reading. In order to keep *1-2-3 Magic* simple and easy to learn, we have not elaborated on certain topics. These topics are listed, and further readings for each are suggested,in the new Appendix.

3. New illustrations (over 90 percent of them).

4. Reorganized parts and new chapters: The old chapter on Stop Behavior and Start Behavior has been included in the new chapter, Your Three Parenting Jobs. The Kickoff Conversation and how to get started have been clarified for each of the three parenting jobs. The Family Meeting

is now part of Chapter 22, Solving Problems Together, and Chapter 21, When Can You Talk?, has been expanded. Chapter 24, Staying on the Wagon, is mostly new, and several chapters in Part IV have new names.

5. Tweens (nine-to-twelve-year-olds) and the issue of kids and technology are on everyone's minds these days. Information relevant to tweens has been included in Chapters 12, More Serious Problems in Tweens, and also in Chapter 23, Kids, Tweens and Tech, which examines our kids' use of cell phones, computers, texting, social networking and so on. As always, we make specific recommendations for handling these situations, some of which may surprise you!

> **Key Concept**
>
> The critical skill of frustration tolerance is encouraged by counting (Parenting Job #1). This, plus the relationship strengthening strategies of Parenting Job #3, is a large part of what emotional intelligence is all about.

6. People have often asked what the relationship is between *1-2-3 Magic* and emotional intelligence. The critical skill of frustration tolerance, encouraged by counting (Parenting Job #1), plus the relationship-strengthening strategies of Parenting Job #3 (especially sympathetic listening) are a large part of what emotional intelligence is all about. Explanations to this effect are included throughout the book.

Our goal for *1-2-3 Magic* is to make a dramatic and positive difference—in a fairly short period of time—in the lives of the parents and other caretakers who use our program, and also in the lives of the children these folks are responsible for. We know you love your kids, but for many reasons it is critically important that you also like and enjoy your children—every day.

Job Available: Long Hours, No Pay Excellent Benefits

Parenting is not for the faint of heart.

"Can I have a Twinkie?"

"No, dear."

"Why not?"

"'Cause we're eating at six o'clock."

"Yeah, but I want one."

"I just told you you couldn't have one."

"You never give me anything."

"What do you mean I never give you anything? Do you have clothes on? Is there a roof over your head? Am I feeding you in two seconds?!"

"You gave Joey one a half-hour ago."

"Listen, are you your brother? Besides, *he* eats his dinner."

"I promise I'll eat my dinner."

"Don't give me this promise, promise, promise stuff, Monica! Yesterday—at 4:30—you had half a peanut butter and jelly sandwich and you didn't eat anything at dinner!"

"THEN I'M GOING TO KILL MYSELF AND THEN RUN AWAY FROM HOME!!"

Welcome to *1-2-3 Magic*

Parenting is one of the most important jobs in the world, and it can also be one of life's most enjoyable experiences. Small children are engaging, affectionate, entertaining, curious, full of life and fun to be around. For many adults, parenting provides profound and unique benefits unequalled by any other area of life.

Yet being a mom or a dad can also be unbelievably frustrating if you don't quite know what you're doing. Repeat the Twinkie scene above a thousand times and you have guaranteed misery. In extreme but all-too-common situations, that misery can become the source of emotional and physical abuse. That's no way for anyone—child or adult—to live.

Children don't come with a How-To-Raise-Me Training Manual. That's why there is a program like *1-2-3 Magic*. The 1-2-3 program is currently being used all over the world by millions of parents (single and divorced), teachers, grandparents, day care centers, babysitters, summer camp counselors, hospital staff and other child caretakers.

The "1-2-3" is also being taught and recommended by thousands of mental health professionals and pediatricians. At parent-teacher conferences, teachers recommend *1-2-3 Magic* to the parents of their students (and sometimes parents recommend *1-2-3 Magic for Teachers* to the teachers!).

Why all the enthusiasm? As one parent put it, "*1-2-3 Magic* was easy to learn and it gave me results. I went back to enjoying my kids and being the kind of mother I knew I could be." Now, at the 25th anniversary of the program, we're hearing from parents who say, "My kids were great kids and now they're nice adults. We enjoy being with them."

1-2-3 Magic helps children grow up to be self-disciplined adults who are competent, happy and able to get along with others. In other words, it helps produce emotionally intelligent people—people who can manage their own feelings as well as understand and respond to the emotions of others.

The methods described in this book are easy to master and *you can start the program right away*. Depending on whether you use the book, audio CD or two DVDs, the technique takes about 3-4 hours to learn. You do not have to be a saint, genius or professional psychotherapist to use the 1-2-3 properly.

How to Get Started

When you finish learning the *1-2-3 Magic* program—whether in book, DVD or audio format—it is a good idea to start immediately. Make sure you understand all three parenting jobs. Talk with your spouse or partner, if both of you are living at home, and then get going right away. If you are a single parent, take a deep breath and then explain the drill to your youngsters. Do the same thing if you're a grandparent. If you don't start right away, you may never get around to it.

Exactly how you start depends on how much energy you have. If you feel like you're barely hanging on by your fingernails, you might want to start with only counting (Parenting Job #1). Then add the good behavior and relationship parts after you're more in control and the kids know you mean business.

If you have more energy, begin with a combination of counting (Chapter 5) and shared fun (Chapter 20). More energetic than that? Start with counting, daily praise and shared fun. See Chapter 9 for more suggestions on getting started with Kickoff Conversations.

> **Quik Tip**
>
> Exactly how you start depends on how much energy you have. If you feel like you're barely hanging on by your fingernails, you might want to start with only counting. Then add the good behavior and relationship steps after the kids know you mean business.

After learning *1-2-3 Magic,* you will know exactly what to do, what not to do, what to say and what not to say in just about every one of the common, everyday problem situations you run into with your kids. Because *1-2-3 Magic* is based on only a few basic but critical principles, you will not only be able to remember what to do, *you will be able to do it when you are anxious, agitated or otherwise upset* (which for many of us parents is every day!). You will also be able to be a kind-but-effective parent when you are busy, in a hurry or otherwise preoccupied.

If you are a mental health professional or pediatrician, suggest that your clients or patients get a copy of the *1-2-3 Magic* book at their local bookstore. Or you can provide them with a copy of the book, DVDs or audio CD. If it's the DVD, make sure you get a deposit or credit card swipe, or else—sooner or later—you'll never see the DVD again!

What to Expect When You Begin the 1-2-3

When you do start *1-2-3 Magic*, things will change quickly. But there is good news and bad news. The good news is that initially about half of all kids will fall into the "immediate cooperator" category. You start the program and they cooperate right away—sometimes "just like magic." What do you do? Just relax and enjoy your good fortune!

The bad news is that the other half of the kids will fall into the "immediate tester" category. These children will get worse first. They will challenge you to see if you really mean business with your new parenting ideas (see Chapter 10, The Six Types of Testing and Manipulation). If you stick to your guns, however—no arguing, yelling or hitting—you will get the vast majority of these little testers shaped up pretty well in about a week to ten days. Then what do you do? You start enjoying your children again.

Believe it or not, you may soon have a much more peaceful home and more enjoyable kids. You will go back to liking and respecting yourself as a parent—all in the foreseeable future!

Before we get into the details of the 1-2-3 and Parenting Job #1, controlling obnoxious behavior, we need to clarify some very important concepts that are the fundamental building blocks of *1-2-3 Magic*:

1. The *most effective orientation to—or philosophy of—parenting* (Chapter 1)
2. The *three basic parenting jobs* (Chapter 2).
3. The *dangerous assumption* parents, teachers and other caretakers make about young children (Chapter 3).
4. The *two biggest discipline mistakes* made by adults (Chapter 4).

Part I
Thinking Straight

Chapter 1

**Orientation to
The Parenting Profession**

Chapter 2

Your Three Parenting Jobs

Chapter 3

The Little Adult Assumption

Chapter 4

The Two Biggest Discipline Mistakes

1

Orientation to
The Parenting Profession

With no training manual, kids come as a bit of a shock.

There's no way you know what parenting is like until you do it. Whatever thoughts you may have had about becoming a mom or a dad, bringing that first child home is a jolt—a big jolt. It's a lot like getting married. Maximum excitement and maximum stress.

1-2-3 Magic is based on the idea that parenting should be looked at as a profession. Some training, in other words, will make the job much easier. But that training shouldn't have to take years or involve bringing tons of books home from the library. One book should do it.

Your Basic Parenting Philosophy

The place to start is with your basic parenting philosophy—your overall orientation to the job. Even though the job changes as the kids get older, effective parents have two important qualities. They are:

1. Warm and friendly on the one hand
2. Demanding and firm on the other

Warm and friendly means taking care of kids' emotional and physical needs. It means feeding them, keeping them safe, warm, well clothed and making sure they get enough sleep. Warmth and friendliness also mean being sensitive to the children's feelings: sharing their joy over a new friend, comforting them when their ice cream falls on the ground, listening sympathetically when they're angry at their teacher, and enjoying their company.

Warm and friendly also means *liking*—not just loving—your children.

Key Concept
Research has shown that effective parents are warm and friendly on the one hand, but also demanding and firm on the other. Both orientations are critical to raising emotionally intelligent and mature kids.

The other important parental trait, *demanding and firm,* is meant in the good sense. Good parents expect something from their kids. They expect good behavior in school, respect toward adults, hard work on academics, effort in sports and relationships with friends that include sharing and kindness. They expect their youngsters to follow the rules, to do things for other people and to sometimes confront issues that are hard or scary.

In other words, effective parents expect their children to rise to life's challenges (as you know, there are plenty!) and to respect the rules and limits that will be required for their behavior.

These two parental orientations, warm/friendly and demanding/firm, might at first seem contradictory. They are not. Some situations call for one, some for the other, and some situations require both. Megan slaps Jon, for example. Time for the demanding side of parenting. Megan feeds the dog without being asked? Time for the warm side.

What if it's time for bed? Both friendly and firm sides are necessary. The friendly side might mean snuggling up in bed with a child for fifteen minutes of storytime before lights out. The demanding side, on the other hand, might mean requiring the kids to get ready for bed (teeth, bath or shower, pajamas, etc.) *before* story time can happen. And at 9 o'clock firm means lights out. No ifs, ands or buts.

The messages this parenting philosophy sends to children are:

1. Warm/friendly: *I love you and I'll take care of you.*
2. Demanding/firm: *I expect something from you.*

Why is the warm and demanding, friendly and firm attitude toward your children the best one? For two reasons. The first reason is simple: fun! It would be nice if you could enjoy the children while they are growing up in your household. Kids are energetic, cute, exciting and fun, and you can have some great times with them you'll never forget.

The second reason is a bit sad: You want your youngsters to grow up, leave home someday and make it on their own. Warm and demanding, therefore, also means *encouraging and respecting your kids' growing independence*. Friendly and firm means not hovering and not being overprotective. It means giving children a chance to do things more and more on their own as they get older. When our oldest walked five blocks to kindergarten the first day of school, I was sure he was never coming back. He came back just fine and I learned a lesson about independence and about his growing competence.

Automatic vs. Deliberate Parenting

You might say there are two kinds of parenting activities: automatic and deliberate. Automatic parenting includes the things you do spontaneously without really thinking (and with no real training), such as picking up and comforting a sobbing two-year-old who has just fallen down. Comforting an upset child is a positive example, but automatic parenting can also include actions that aren't so hot, such as screaming at a seven-year-old who keeps getting out of bed because she says she hears a noise in her closet.

Here's what you'll want to do with the *1-2-3 Magic* program. First, hang on to your positive automatic parenting habits. You'll find that some of your beneficial parenting moves are already part of the program, such as being a good listener or praising your kids' efforts.

Next, identify your automatic parenting habits that are harmful, useless or upsetting. As you read through *1-2-3 Magic*, decide how you'll replace these negative actions with deliberate, respectful and more useful *1-2-3 Magic* strategies. You might, for example, replace yelling about whining with *counting* whining; you might also consider replacing nagging and arguing at 9 p.m. with the *Basic Bedtime Method*.

Finally, practice, practice, practice! Work hard and thoughtfully until the new methods become more or less automatic. Because *1-2-3 Magic* works so well, it tends to be self-reinforcing, which makes the deliberate-to-automatic conversion much easier.

Quik Tip

Identify your automatic parenting habits that are harmful, useless or upsetting, and as you read *1-2-3 Magic*, decide how you'll replace these negative actions with deliberate, respectful and more useful strategies.

Automatic parenting includes another critically important activity that you do all the time: *modeling*. Children are great imitators, and they learn a lot by just watching the way you behave. If you are respectful toward others, your kids will tend to be the same. If you scream in fury during fits of road-rage, on the other hand ... well, you get the idea.

The goal, therefore, is effective, automatic parenting. It takes some concentration and effort in the beginning, but in the end it's a whole lot less work. And you and your family are a whole lot better off!

CHAPTER SUMMARY

WARM FRIENDLY   DEMANDING FIRM

2

Your Three Parenting Jobs

It's always helpful to have a good job description.

We have three separate parenting jobs, and these three jobs require different strategies. Each of the three parenting jobs is distinct, manageable and important. The three parenting steps are also inter-dependent; each depends to some extent on the others for its success. Ignore any of these tasks at your own risk! Do these three tasks well and you'll be a pretty good mom or dad. The first two parenting jobs involve discipline/behavior concerns, and the third job focuses on the parent/child relationship.

Parenting Job #1 (Parts II and III in the book) involves *controlling obnoxious behavior*. You will never like or get along well with your children if they are constantly irritating you with behavior such as whining, arguing, teasing, badgering, tantrums, yelling and fighting. In *1-2-3 Magic* you will learn how to "count" obnoxious behavior, and you will be pleasantly surprised at how effective that simple technique is!

Job #2 (Part IV) involves *encouraging good behavior*. Encouraging good behavior, such as picking up after yourself, going to bed, being courteous and doing homework, takes more effort—for both parent and child—than controlling difficult behavior. You will learn seven simple methods for encouraging positive actions in your kids.

Finally, in Part V you will learn some valuable and not-so-difficult ways of handling Parenting Job #3: *strengthening your relationship with your children.* Some parents merely need to be reminded of Parenting Job #3; other parents have to work hard at remembering to do it. Paying attention to the quality of your relationship with your children will help you with jobs 1 and 2, and vice versa.

Quik Tip

Some parents only need a simple reminder about Parenting Job #3: strengthening your relationship with your children. Other parents, however, have to work hard at remembering to do it.

How do our three parenting jobs relate to the warm/demanding parenting traits? As you may have guessed already, the tactic for Job #1, controlling obnoxious behavior, depends almost entirely on the demanding parent role. Not much warm or fuzzy about it! Job #3, however, strengthening relationships, will rely almost entirely on the warm side of the parenting equation. And finally, Job #2, encouraging good behavior, will employ both warm as well as demanding strategies.

Parenting Jobs #1 and #2: "Stop" vs. "Start" Behavior

When it comes to discipline, there are two basic problems children present to adults, and these two problems define the first two parenting tasks. When we are frustrated with our youngsters, the kids are either (1) doing something negative we want them to *Stop* (like whining), or (2) they are not doing something positive we would like them to *Start* (like getting dressed). In *1-2-3 Magic*, therefore, we call these two kinds of things "Stop" behavior and "Start" behavior. In the hustle and bustle of everyday existence, you may not have worried much about the difference between Start and Stop behaviors, but—as we'll soon see—the distinction is extremely important. This distinction is also about to make your life a lot easier!

Stop behavior includes frequent, minor, everyday issues, such as whining, disrespect, tantrums, arguing, teasing, fighting, pouting, yelling and so on. Stop behavior—in and of itself—ranges from mildly irritating to pretty obnoxious. Each of these difficult behaviors alone may not be so bad, but add them all up in one afternoon and by 5 p.m. you may feel like hitchhiking to South America.

Start behavior includes positive activities like cleaning rooms, doing homework, practicing the piano, getting up and out in the morning, going to bed, eating supper and being nice to other people. You have a Start behavior problem when your child is not doing something that would be a good thing to do. The reason for distinguishing between Stop and Start behavior is this: You will use different tactics for each kind of problem.

For Stop behavior, such as whining, arguing, screaming and teasing, you will use the 1-2-3, or "counting" procedure. Counting is simple, gentle and direct. For Start behavior problems, you will have a choice of seven tactics, which can be used either one at a time or in combination. These tactics include Praise, Simple Requests, Kitchen Timers, The Docking System, Natural Consequences, Charting and Counting Variation. Start behavior strategies, as you can probably guess, require a little more thought and effort than counting does.

Important Reminder

For **Stop behavior**, such as:	For **Start behavior**, such as:
Whining	Picking up
Teasing	Eating
Arguing	Homework
Pouting	Bedtime
Yelling	Up and out
Tantrums	
Etc.	Use Praise, Simple Requests, Kitchen Timers, The Docking System, Natural Consequences, Charting and the Counting Variation.
Use the 1-2-3, or "counting" procedure.	

Why the difference in strategies? The answer lies in the issue of motivation. How long does it take a child—if she is motivated—to terminate an irritating (Stop) behavior like whining, arguing or teasing? The answer is about one second; it's really not a big project. Depending on how angry or oppositional a child is, ending an obnoxious behavior doesn't take tons of effort.

But now look at Start behavior. How long does it take a child to accomplish something constructive like eating dinner? Maybe twenty to twenty-five minutes. To pick up after himself? Perhaps fifteen minutes. To get ready for bed? Twenty to thirty minutes. Ready for school? Thirty minutes. Homework? Schoolwork might take anywhere from forty minutes to three years. So it's obvious that with Start behavior, more motivation is required from the child. He has to begin the project, keep at it and then finish. And the project is often something the boy or girl is not thrilled about having to do in the first place.

In addition, if encouraging positive behavior in kids requires more motivation in the kids, it's also going to require more motivation from Mom and Dad. As you'll soon see, putting an end to Stop behavior using counting is relatively easy if you do it right. Start behavior is harder.

When managing a behavioral difficulty with one of your children, therefore, you will need to first determine if you have a Stop or a Start behavior problem. "Is the issue something I want the child to quit? Or is it something I want the youngster to get going on?" Since counting is so easy, parents sometimes make the mistake of using counting for Start behavior (for example, counting a child to get her to do her homework). As you will soon see, counting produces motivation that usually lasts only a short time (from a few seconds to a couple of minutes) in children. If you mix up your tactics (such as using counting for homework), you will not get optimum results.

But don't worry. This whole procedure is so simple, you'll be an expert in no time. Effective discipline will start to come naturally and—believe it or not—your kids will start listening to you.

Parenting Job #3

Your final parenting job is to work on strengthening your relationship with your kids. This means making sure that screen time does not replace face-to-face time, and—more importantly—strengthening relationships means that you value enjoying one another's company. It is critical to your family's well being and to your kids' self-esteem that you like (not just love) your youngsters.

What does "like" mean? Here's an example. It's a Saturday and you're home by yourself for a few hours—a rare occurrence! Everyone has gone out. You're listening to some music and just puttering around. You hear a noise outside and look out to see a car pulling up in the driveway. One of your kids gets out and heads for the front door.

How do you feel in your gut right at that moment? If it's "Oh no, the fun's over!" that may not be *like*. If it's "Oh good, I've got some company!" that's more like *like*.

Liking your children and having a good relationship with them is important for lots of reasons. The most important reason, though, may be that it's simply more fun. Kids are naturally cute and enjoyable a lot of the time, and you want to take advantage of that valuable quality. And they only grow up with you once.

In *1-2-3 Magic* we'll discuss four strategies for strengthening relationships:

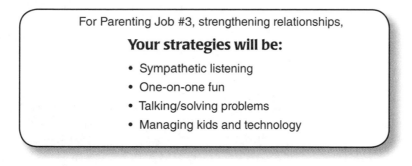

For Parenting Job #3, strengthening relationships,

Your strategies will be:

- Sympathetic listening
- One-on-one fun
- Talking/solving problems
- Managing kids and technology

Next up? In Chapter 3 we'll examine the strange and amazingly disruptive idea that adults carry around in their brains about small children.

3

The Little Adult Assumption

How many times do I have to tell you!

There is an enchanting, semi-conscious and trouble-producing idea that parents and teachers carry around in their heads about young children. This naive assumption—or wish—causes not only discipline failures, but also stormy scenes that can include physical child abuse. The idea we're talking about is known as the "Little Adult Assumption."

The Little Adult Assumption is the belief that kids have hearts of gold and are basically reasonable and unselfish. In other words, they're just smaller versions of grownups. And because they are little adults, the idea goes, whenever the youngsters are misbehaving, the problem must be that they don't have enough information in their heads to be able to do the right thing. The solution? Simply give them the facts.

Imagine, for example, that at exactly 4:12 p.m. your eight-year-old son is teasing his five-year-old sister for the eighteenth time since they got home from school. What should you do? If your boy is a little adult, you simply sit him down, calmly look him in the eye, and explain to him the three golden reasons why he shouldn't tease his sister. First of all, teasing hurts her. Second, it makes you mad at him. Third—and most important—how would he feel if someone treated him like that?

Now imagine further that after this explanation your son looks at you—his face brightening with insight—and he says, "Gee, I never looked at it like that before!" Then he stops bothering his sibling for the rest of his life. That would certainly be nice, but any veteran parent or teacher knows that doesn't happen. Kids are not little adults.

The crucial point here is this: Grownups who want to believe the Little Adult Assumption are going to rely heavily on *words and reasons* in dealing with young kids. And words and reasons, by themselves, are going to be miserable failures much of the time. Sometimes explanations will have absolutely no impact at all. At other times adult attempts at enlightenment will take parent and child through what we call the *Talk-Per-suade-Argue-Yell-Hit Syndrome.*

> **Quik Tip**
> Adults who believe in the Little Adult Assumption are going to rely heavily on words and reasons in trying to change the behavior of young kids. And words and reasons are going to be miserable failures much of the time.

Your child is doing something you don't like. A parenting book said you should talk the problem out no matter how long it takes. So you try telling your five-year-old daughter why she shouldn't be disrespectful. She doesn't respond, so you next try to persuade her to see things your way. When persuasion fails, you start arguing. Arguing leads to a yelling match, and when that fails, you may feel there is nothing left to do but hit.

Actually, the vast majority of the time when parents scream, hit and spank their children, the parent is simply having a temper tantrum. The tantrum is a sign that 1) the parent doesn't know what to do, 2) the parent is so frustrated that he or she can't see straight, and 3) this adult may have an anger management problem.

We're not implying that you are going around hitting your kids all the time. It may be true, however, that the chief cause of child abuse (physical abuse, not sexual) is the Little Adult Assumption. A parent reads in a book that reasoning is the preferred method. When reasoning fails, however, the parent goes crazy and starts hitting, because his favorite strategy isn't working and desperation has set in.

Talking and explaining certainly have their place in raising children (see Chapter 21, When Can You Talk?). But kids are just kids—not little adults. Years ago one writer said, "Childhood is a period of transitory psychosis." She meant that kids, when they are little, are—in a way—basically nuts! They are not born reasonable and unselfish, they are born unreasonable and selfish. They want what they want when they want it, and they can have a major fit if they don't get it. Consequently, it is the parent's job—and the teacher's job—to help kids gradually learn frustration tolerance. In accomplishing this goal, adults need to be gentle, consistent, decisive and calm.

How do you do that? You start by changing your thinking about children and by getting rid of the Little Adult Assumption. In order to get this crazy and harmful notion out of parents' heads, we use a bit of what we call "cognitive shock therapy." Although it may sound strange, think of it like this: Instead of imagining your kids as little adults, think of yourself as a *wild animal trainer*! Of course, we don't mean using whips, guns or chairs. And we certainly don't mean being nasty.

CAUTION
One explanation, if really necessary, is fine. It's the attempts at *repeated explanations* that get adults and kids into trouble. Too much parent talking irritates and distracts children.

But what does a wild animal trainer do? He chooses a method—which is largely nonverbal—and repeats it until the "trainee" does what the trainer wants. The trainer is patient, gentle and persistent. Our job in *1-2-3 Magic* is to present some training methods to you, so that you can repeat them until the trainees, your children, do what you want them to.

Fortunately, you do not usually have to repeat these methods for very long before you get results. And you can gradually add more talking and reasoning as the kids get older. But remember this: One explanation—if necessary—is fine. It's the attempts at repeated explanations that get adults and children in trouble.

Dictatorship to Democracy

The overall orientation of *1-2-3 Magic* is what you might call "dictatorship to democracy." When your kids are little, your house should be pretty much a benign dictatorship where you are the judge and jury. Your four-year-old, for example, cannot unilaterally choose—at 7:30 in the morning on Wednesday—to skip preschool because she wants to stay home and play with her new birthday stuff.

When the kids are in their mid to late teens, however, your house should be more of a democracy. The youngsters should have more say about the rules that affect them. You should have family meetings to iron out differences. Even when the kids are teens, though, when push comes to shove, who's paying the mortgage? You are. And who knows better than the kids do what's good for them? You do. And, when necessary, you have a right—and a duty—to impose limits on your children, even if they don't like it.

> **Key Concept**
>
> Noncompliance and lack of cooperation in children are not always due to lack of information. Kids are not little adults or simply small computers, so raising youngsters involves training as well as explaining.

Too many parents these days are afraid of their children. What are they afraid of? Physical attack? Not usually. What many parents fear is that their children won't like them. So, in a conflict situation, these parents explain and explain and explain, hoping the child will eventually come around and say something like, "Gee, I never looked at it like that before." All too often, these parental efforts simply lead to the Talk-Persuade-Argue-Yell or Talk-Persuade-Argue-Yell-Hit Syndrome.

What if you have children who always respond to words and reasons? You are certainly lucky! Recent research has indicated that there are three such children in the country. If you have one or more of them, you may not need this book. Or, if your kids stop responding to logic, you can consider using the 1-2-3.

So what is the training method we're talking about? We first have to explain what it is not.

CHAPTER SUMMARY

What's wrong with this picture?

4

The Two Biggest Discipline Mistakes

Chatter, chatter, chatter, chatter — boom, boom, boom.

The two biggest discipline mistakes that parents and other caretakers make in dealing with young children are 1) too much talking and 2) too much emotion. Thinking of kids as little adults and then chattering away in a discipline situation is bad because excessive explaining makes kids *less likely to cooperate* by irritating, confusing and distracting them. Endless chatter also leads to the Talk-Persuade-Argue-Yell-Hit Syndrome.

But why is too much adult emotion bad during discipline? People today tell you to "let it all hang out" and show your feelings. "Express yourself and don't keep it all inside" seems to be the universal recommendation of modern psychology.

Is this a good suggestion if you are a parent? One-half of it is good advice and the other half is not. The good half is this: If you are feeling positively toward a child, by all means let it show. Express your affection or dole out some praise. You are not going to do anything harmful, and you will do some good.

The bad half of the let-it-all-hang-out advice, though, applies to times when you are irritated or angry with your children. Cutting loose at these moments can be a problem, because when we parents are mad we often do the wrong thing. Angry adults can yell, scream, belittle and nag; they can also physically endanger their kids. *1-2-3 Magic* is as much a control on parental anger as it is a control on children's behavior.

The Big Splash!

There is another reason why too much emotion can interfere with effective parenting and effective teaching. When they are little, kids feel inferior. They feel inferior because they *are* inferior. They are smaller, less privileged, less intelligent, less skillful, less responsible and less of just about everything than their parents and the older kids are. And this "lessness" bugs them a lot. They don't like it. They do like to feel they are powerful and capable of making some mark on the world.

Quik Tip
If your little child can get big-old you all upset, your upset is the big splash for him. Your emotional outburst accidentally makes your child feel powerful.

Watch your two-year-olds. They want to be like those cool five-year-olds, who can do a lot more neat things. The five-year-olds, in turn, want to be like the cool ten-year-olds. And the ten-year-olds want to be like you; they want to drive cars and use cell phones and credit cards (and some do!). They want to have an impact on the world and to make things happen.

Have you ever seen a small child go down to a lake and throw rocks in the water? Children can do that for hours, partly because the big splashes are a sign of their impact. They are the ones causing all the commotion.

"What does this have to do with what happens at my house?" you may ask. Simple. If your little child can get big-old you all upset, *your upset is the big splash for him*. Your emotional outburst accidentally makes your child feel powerful. His reaction does not mean that he has no conscience or is going to grow up to be a professional criminal. It's just a normal childhood feeling: Having all that power temporarily rewards—or feels good to—the inferior part of the child. Parents who say, "It drives me absolutely crazy when she eats her dinner with her fingers!! Why does she do that?!" may have already answered their own question. She may do that—at least partly—*because it drives Mom and Dad crazy*.

An important rule, therefore, is this: If you have a child who is doing something you don't like, get real upset about it on a regular basis and, sure enough, she'll repeat it for you.

When it comes to discipline, you want to be consistent, decisive and calm. So what we recommend in *1-2-3 Magic* is that you apply—during moments involving conflict or discipline—what we call the "No-Talking and No-Emotion" Rules. Since we're all human, these two rules really mean very little talking and very little emotion. *But these rules are absolutely critical to your disciplinary effectiveness.* There are discipline systems other than the 1-2-3, but you will ruin any of them by talking too much and getting too excited. These two mistakes, of course, usually go hand in hand, and the emotion involved is usually anger.

Some parents and teachers can turn off the talking and the emotional upset like a faucet, especially once they see how effective it is to keep quiet at the right time. Other adults, however, have to bite their lips bloody to get the job done. I saw a T-shirt a while back that said, "Help me—I'm talking and I can't stop!" Lots of moms, dads and teachers have to remind themselves over and over and over again that talking, arguing, yelling and screaming not only don't help, they actually make things worse. These "tactics" merely blow off steam for a few seconds. If, after a month to six weeks of using *1-2-3 Magic*, parents find that they can't shake these habits, it's time to face facts: Some sort of outpatient evaluation and counseling is indicated (for the adult, not the child!).

Remember, we're talking here primarily about negative or angry emotion and talk—not positive. Good parents do express warmth and affection for their kids. They do listen sympathetically when the children are upset. It's discipline and parent/child conflict situations where you really have to watch yourself.

CHAPTER SUMMARY

Too Much Talking
Too Much Emotion

Part II

Controlling Obnoxious Behavior
(Job #1)

5

Counting: Simple But Not Easy!

Sometimes your silence speaks louder than your words.

When your kids are acting up, you now know what you're not supposed to do: get excited and start chattering. But just what *are* you supposed to do?

To help with your first giant parenting job—controlling obnoxious behavior—you'll use the 1-2-3, or counting procedure. Counting is surprisingly powerful and deceptively simple, but you have to know what you're doing. In the beginning, keep two things in mind.

First, you will use the counting method to deal with Stop (obnoxious or difficult) behavior. In other words, you will be counting things like arguing, fighting, whining, yelling, tantrums, etc. You will not use the 1-2-3 to get the child up in the morning, to get her to do her homework or to motivate her to practice the piano.

Second, if you are new to *1-2-3 Magic*, after you hear how to do the 1-2-3, you will be skeptical. The procedure will seem too easy; it may not appear aggressive or tough enough. Some of you will think, "Hey, you don't know my kid. This kid is a wild man!"

Don't worry about feeling skeptical. Remember the 1-2-3 *is* simple, but it is not always easy. The "magic" is not in the counting. Anyone can count. The magic—or what may seem like magic after you've done it for a while—is in the No-Talking and No-Emotion Rules. Your following these rules makes children think and take responsibility for their own behavior.

Of course, there really is no magic in *1-2-3 Magic*. It just seems that way. The program represents the careful, logical and persistent extension of a special behavioral technology to the gentle discipline and training of children. Soon—when conflicts with kids arise—you will feel like a new person: consistent, decisive and calm.

Undoubtedly, after our initial explanation, you will have questions. We will attempt to answer all of your questions in the next chapter. After that, and after you have read through the information in Chapters 6-12, you can begin counting.

Introduction to Counting

How does the 1-2-3 work? Imagine you have a four-year-old child (some of you don't have to imagine!). This child is having a major temper tantrum on the kitchen floor at 6 p.m. because you—in your hardness of heart—would not give him a small bag of potato chips right before dinner. Your son is banging his head on the floor, kicking your new kitchen cabinets, and screaming bloody murder. You are sure the neighbors can hear the noise all the way down the block, and you're at a loss for what to do.

Your pediatrician told you to ignore your son's temper tantrums, but you don't think you can stand it. Your mother told you to put a cold washcloth on the youngster's face, but you think her advice is strange. And, finally, your husband told you to spank the boy.

None of these is an acceptable alternative. Instead, you hold up one finger, look down at your noisy little devil, and calmly say, "That's 1."

He doesn't care. He's insane with rage and keeps the tantrum going full blast. You let five seconds go by, then you hold up two fingers and say, "That's 2." That's all you say. But you get the same lousy reaction; the tantrum continues. So after five more seconds, you hold up three fingers and say, "That's 3, take 5."

Now what does all this mean? It means that your son was just given two chances—the first two counts—to shape up. But in this instance he blew it—he didn't shape up. So there is going to be a consequence. The consequence can be a "rest period" or "time-out" (about one minute per year of the child's life), or the consequence can be what we call a "time-out alternative" (loss of a privilege or toy for a period of time, bedtime fifteen minutes earlier, twenty-five cents off the allowance, no electronic entertainment for two hours, etc.)

Let's imagine the consequence you choose is a rest period or time-out. (Time-outs work just fine, by the way, if they are administered fairly by non-tantruming adults.) After you say "That's 3, take 5," the child goes to time-out. (Some of you are wondering, "How do I get him there?" That question will be answered in the next chapter.)

After the time-out is served, you will not believe what happens next. Nothing! No talking, no emotion, no apologies, no lectures, no discussions. Nothing is said unless it is absolutely necessary, which is usually not the case.

Quik Tip

What is going to happen, in a relatively short period of time, is this: You'll start getting good control—believe it or not—at 1 or 2. And that is going to make you feel real good!

You do not say, for example, "Now, are you going to be a good boy? Do you realize what you've been doing to your mother all afternoon?! Why do we have to go through this all the time? I'm so sick and tired of this I could scream!! Your sister doesn't behave this way and your father's coming home in half an hour. Did God put you on earth to drive me crazy or what?!"

Tempting as this lecture might be, you simply keep quiet. If the child behaves, praise him and enjoy his company. If the child does something else that's countable, count it.

What is going to happen, in a relatively short period of time, is this: You'll start getting good control—believe it or not—at 1 or 2. And we will promise you this: The first time you stop a fight between two of your kids across fifteen feet of living room, and all you have to do is say, "That's 1" or "That's 2," and you don't have to get up or yell or scream or do something worse that you'll be sorry for later ... the first time you do that, you're going to feel real good!

Some parents ask, "My child always takes us to 2. Don't you think he's manipulating us?" The answer is, "No, he's not necessarily manipulating you by always taking you to 2." Why? Because what really drives people crazy is 42! Or 72—a child who has to be told a thousand times before he'll shape up. Two times is not so bad. Remember, if the child hits 3, that's it.

Other parents ask, with good reason, "What if my son or daughter does something that's so bad I don't want to give them three chances to do it?" That's a good question. For example, what if your child hits you? Your kids can't hit you. If your child hits you, it would be ridiculous to say, "That's 1," and give him two more chances to sock away. So if in your opinion the behavior is bad enough to begin with, you simply say, "That's 3, take 5 and add 15 more for the seriousness of the offense."

Let's look at another example. What if your seven-year-old learns a bad word on the playground? He doesn't know what it means, but he wants to try it out on you. So at 8:30 when you say it's time to get ready for bed, he replies, "You blankity-blank!" Same thing. "That's 3, take 5, and add 15 more for the rotten mouth." And in this example, when that youngster returns from time-out, a short explanation will be in order concerning what the word meant and why he can't use it in your house. Remember: Explanations are appropriate when a child's misbehavior is new, unusual or dangerous.

That's it. That's the essence of counting. Counting is extremely simple, direct and effective. You are thinking that there must be a catch. There is.

The Not-So-Easy Part

Occasionally I have run into parents who say this to me: "We went to your workshop about eight weeks ago and we enjoyed it. We have two fairly difficult kids, aged seven and five. When we went home we were very surprised. *1-2-3 Magic* worked and our children were much better behaved. But that was two months ago. The 1-2-3 is not working anymore. We need a new discipline program."

What's the problem here? Ninety percent of the time—not all the time—the problem is that the parents "forgot" the No-Talking and No-Emotion rules. Adults can slip up like this *without even being aware of it.*

Remember our four-year-old tantrum artist and the potato chips? Here's how that scene might sound if the parent is unwittingly talking too much and getting too excited while attempting to count the child's outburst:

> "That's 1. Come on now, I'm getting a little tired of
> this. Why can't you do one little thing for us—LOOK
> AT ME WHEN I'M TALKING TO YOU, YOUNG MAN!
> OK, that's 2. One more and you're going to your room, do
> you hear me? I'm sick and tired of you whining and
> fussing over every little thing you can't have. One more and
> that's it. YOUR SISTER NEVER BEHAVES THIS WAY ...
> YOUR FATHER'S COMING HOME IN HALF AN HOUR!
> OK, ENOUGH! THAT'S 3, TAKE 5. BEAT IT! OUT OF
> MY SIGHT!!'"

What was that? That was a parental temper tantrum. Now we have two tantrums going on in the same kitchen. This adult's outburst was not the 1-2-3 at all. What's wrong with what this angry parent just did? Three things.

First of all, do you want to talk to a child like that? Did you have a bad day at the office? If you do "communicate" like this parent just did, what you are really saying is simply this: "Let's fight!" And you don't have to have an ADHD kid or an ODD (Oppositional Defiant) kid or a CD (Conduct Disorder) kid—you're going to get a fight. There are plenty of kids who would rather cut off their left leg than lose a good battle of words. Unwise attempts at talking or persuading are guaranteed to take a child's focus *off* the possibility of good behavior and put it *on* the prospect of an enjoyable and energetic argument.

Key Concept
Talk too much and you switch your child's focus off the need for good behavior and on to the possibility of an enjoyable argument. There are plenty of kids who would rather cut off their left leg than lose a good battle of words.

Second, many difficult children do have Attention Deficit Disorder. That doesn't mean they don't *get* enough attention. It means they can't *pay* attention. How is an ADHD child, or any other youngster for that matter, supposed to pick out—from that huge mass of adult words—

the most important parts, which are the counts or warnings? He can't. Children can't respond properly to warnings if they don't hear them clearly in the first place.

Finally, there is a third thing wrong with our super-frustrated parent's message. Even if you forget all the emotion involved, as Mom or Dad talks more and more, their basic message changes. When a parent gives lots and lots of reasons to a child regarding why he should shape up, the real message becomes: "You don't have to behave unless I can give you five or six good reasons why you should. And, gee whiz, I certainly hope you agree with my reasons." This is not discipline. The word describing this "strategy" starts with the letter B. It's *begging*. When you beg like this, you are 1) trying to think for your child, 2) taking the responsibility for his behavior, and 3) really caught up in the Little Adult Assumption.

What's the average child going to do? He's going to take issue with your reasons. "Katie doesn't always do what you say. Daddy's not coming home in half an hour." Now you have, in effect, left the discipline ballpark and you're out in the street arguing. The main issue has been forgotten. What is the main issue? "Is the child behaving?" is the main issue.

So if the child is acting up, it's "That's 1" (bite your tongue). Then, if necessary, "That's 2" (easy does it, keep quiet), and so on. Count firmly but respectfully; your voice can be casual or even a little stern. Remember that the magic is not in the counting, it's in the *pregnant pause right after the warning*. In that moment—if the adult keeps still—the responsibility for the child's behavior falls squarely on the youngster's own shoulders. You wouldn't want it any other way.

When it comes to counting, your silence will speak louder than your words.

Our Famous Twinkie Example

Our Famous Twinkie Example will help you better understand the workings of the 1-2-3. This is a situation almost all parents have experienced at one time or another. Mom is cooking dinner at 5:45 p.m. and her eight-year-old daughter walks into the kitchen:

"Can I have a Twinkie?"

"No, dear."

"Why not?"

"Because we're eating at six o'clock."

Is there anything wrong with this conversation? No. The child asks a clear question and the parent gives a clear answer. The problem, however, is that some kids won't leave it there; they will press the issue further by adding, in a whiny voice, "Yeah, but I want one."

What is this parent going to do now? She's a little aggravated and she's already given the necessary explanation. Should she repeat herself? Elaborate on her answer? Keep quiet? Give a reprimand?

Let's play this situation through in three scenes. In Scene I, we'll have starring for us a mother who believes that kids are little adults and that words and reasons will work everything out. We'll see what happens with that approach.

Then, in Scene II, our mother will be getting smarter. She will be starting to use counting, but the child won't be used to it yet.

In Scene III, the mother will be using the 1-2-3 and her daughter will be used to it.

Scene I– Starring the Mother Who Believes Kids Are Little Adults:

"Can I have a Twinkie?"

"No, dear."

"Why not?"

"'Cause we're eating at six o'clock."

"Yeah, but I want one."

"I just told you you couldn't have one."

"You never give me anything."

"What do you mean I never give you anything? Do you have clothes on? Is there a roof over your head? Am I feeding you in two seconds?!"

"You gave Joey one a half-hour ago."

"Listen, are you your brother? And besides, *he* eats his dinner."

"I promise I'll eat my dinner."

"Don't give me this promise, promise, promise stuff, Monica!
  Yesterday—4:30 in the afternoon—you had half a peanut
  butter and jelly sandwich and you didn't eat anything at dinner!"
"THEN I'M GOING TO KILL MYSELF AND THEN
  RUN AWAY FROM HOME!!"
"WELL, BE MY GUEST. I'M SICK OF THIS!!"

You can see where trying to talk at the wrong time can get you.
Though everything Mom said was true, her talking made things worse.

In the next scene, Mom is getting smarter and starting to use the
1-2-3, but it's new and the child is still getting used to it.

Scene II—Starring the Mother Beginning the 1-2-3:

"Can I have a Twinkie?"
"No, dear."
"Why not?"
"Because we're eating at
  six o'clock."
"Yeah, but I want one."
"That's 1."
"You never give me anything!"
"That's 2."
"THEN I'M GOING TO KILL MYSELF AND THEN RUN
  AWAY FROM HOME!!"
"That's 3, take 5."

Mom did much better. The temporarily unhappy child disappears
for a rest period and the episode is over.

How's it going to go when the child is more used to counting and
realizes that testing and manipulation are useless?

Scene III—The 1-2-3 After the Child's Used to It:

"Can I have a Twinkie?"
"No, dear."
"Why not?"

"Because we're eating at six o'clock."

"Yeah, but I want one."

"That's 1."

(Pause) "Oh, all right." (Grumpy exit from kitchen)

Good work by Mom again. She doesn't have to count the grumpy "Oh, all right" because the comment is minor and the child is leaving the scene of the crime. If the child had said, "Oh, all right, you stupid jerk!" there would be an automatic 3 and the girl would be off to her room for a longer time-out.

Is ignoring the child's badgering an option? Perhaps, if (1) the child quickly gets the message and drops the issue and if (2) the parent can stand it. But in general—and especially in the beginning—counting is best.

The Benefits of Counting

There are a lot of benefits to using the 1-2-3 to manage difficult childhood behavior. Here are just a few of them.

Energy savings!

The 1-2-3 will save you a lot of breath—and a lot of aggravation. Parents and teachers say counting makes discipline a whole lot less exhausting. Give one explanation, if absolutely necessary, and then count. No extra talking and no extra emotion. You stay calmer and you feel better—about your child and yourself—when you get a good response at 1 or 2.

When is an explanation or more talking absolutely necessary? In those instances when the problem involved is something new that the child does not understand, when what he did is something that is unusual or dangerous, or when you really need more information from him about what happened.

Quik Tip

Give one explanation, if absolutely necessary, and then count. No extra talking and no extra emotion. You stay calmer and you feel better.

Here's an example. Your seven-year-old son has been learning trampoline in gym class and he loves it. After school he comes home, takes off his shoes, and attacks the couch in the living room. He's jumping up and down and trying to do flips. You enter the room, see what's going on and are somewhat startled. You say, "That's 1." Your son says, "What did I do?"

Is an explanation in order? Yes. He's never been trampolining on your couch before. You tell him that although he took off his shoes, which you appreciate, you're afraid he'll hurt himself or ruin the couch and that's why you counted. Good explanation.

When is an explanation not necessary? Imagine that a few hours later on the same day, the same seven-year-old—for no apparent reason—gives his younger sister a medium-sized shove right in front of you. You say, "That's 1." He growls, "WHAT DID I DO?!" You say, "That's 2." This is pure defiance and it is not a real question. Do you need to explain that he just shoved his sister? Of course not. There were three witnesses. An explanation here would simply invite the boy to argue with you. And this kid sounds like he's ready for an argument! Argue back and you have just left the discipline ballpark again.

More affection, more fun

It's sad to say, but in many families careless attempts at discipline take up lots and lots of time. The Talk-Persuade-Argue-Yell—and sometimes Hit—Syndrome can run its course in less than a minute, but it can also occupy hours and hours. During this time everyone is agitated and angry. Parents do not like their kids and kids do not like their parents.

With the 1-2-3, the issue is usually settled in a matter of seconds. Are the children frustrated when they are counted and don't get their way? Of course, but they get over it more quickly than they would if you and they just spent an hour or so trying to persuade, argue and yell each other into submission. After counting, things quickly go back to normal. You can enjoy your kids and they can enjoy you. There is not only more *time* for fun and affection, but you also *feel* more like having fun and being affectionate.

Your authority is not negotiable

You would go crazy if you had to negotiate—every day—issues like getting up, going to school, going to bed, homework, whining and sibling rivalry. You are the boss. As a matter of fact, as a parent you must frustrate your kids on a regular basis, because you can't possibly give them everything they want. But you want to be a nice boss.

Many parents, though, complicate their job of discipline by trying to be too nice. In other words, they set two goals for themselves instead of just one. Their first goal is to discipline their children, which is fine. But their second goal is *to get the kids to like it!* Like the mother in Scene I of The Famous Twinkie Example, the parents talk and talk and talk, waiting for the youngsters to say something like, "Gee, I never looked at it like that before. Thanks for taking the time to explain it to me. I appreciate your efforts to raise me to be a responsible child."

Let's get real. There's the Little Adult Assumption lurking in the back of the parental brain again. If your child does listen all the time and more talking seems to help, fine. You're lucky. But with frustrated children that is not usually the case; too often all that talking escalates to arguing and worse.

The punishment is short and sweet

1-2-3 Magic is a control on the kids, but it's also a control on the parents. As a parent, it's not always easy to be reasonable, especially when you're angry. These days there is an argument about the use of punishment in raising kids. Some vote for no punishment at all, some vote for limited punishment, and, sadly, some parents are just plain brutal.

I saw a mother once who was court-ordered to see me; it was see me or go to jail. This was because she had poured Drano down her four-year-old's throat once when the child talked back to her. I also knew a father who set fire to his daughter's doll in the kitchen sink (after dousing the thing with lighter fluid) after a long argument about homework. These are examples of cruel, unusual and stupid punishments.

Though the vast majority of parents will never come close to taking such ridiculous and nasty measures, they may still be vulnerable to episodes of yelling, name-calling, belittling or even rough physical tactics. But with *1-2-3 Magic* the consequences are reasonable, well-defined, and just potent enough to do the job: A rest period or time-out lasts approximately one minute per year of the child's life. Time-out alternatives, such as a fifty-cent fine or a brief chore, can also be considered.

Are time-outs and time-out alternatives punishments? Yes. But they are not cruel, unusual or stupid. A time-out is also a chance for everyone to calm down. These brief and reasonable consequences do not make the child so mad that he wants war. With this regimen, for example, most kids come back from time-out having forgotten about the whole thing. And your not being allowed to bring up and rehash what happened—unless absolutely necessary—also helps the house *quickly* return to normal.

So what's the bottom line: Is there a role for punishment in raising children? Yes, but mild, reasonable punishment administered by a non-tantruming parent.

Easy for other caretakers to learn

The 1-2-3 is also easy enough to learn that you can train babysitters, grandparents and other caretakers to use it. Parents who are using the 1-2-3 at home often tell their child's teachers about the program. In turn, teachers who use *1-2-3 Magic* in class often share the idea with parents who are struggling with their child's behavior at home.

When kids get the same message from everyone at home and at school, this cross-situation consistency makes the program much more powerful and easier for the children to learn. "That's 1," whether at home or at school, means "You're doing something wrong and it's time to shape up."

We have found that home/school coordination of the 1-2-3 is especially helpful with behaviorally difficult children. When both parents and teachers use counting fairly and consistently, and when they also respect the No-Talking and No-Emotion rules, we have seen positive revolutions take place in the behavior of some very challenging kids.

Time-Out Alternatives (TOAs)

For various reasons, there may be times when you do not want to use a time-out as the consequence for a child's arriving at a count of 3. Perhaps there isn't time for a rest period when you're dashing out the door in the morning, perhaps you feel you want a consequence with a little more clout, or perhaps you want a consequence that fits the crime. The judicious use of time-out alternatives can be of great value. Here are some TOA possibilities:

Earlier bedtime	Loss of TV for evening
Loss of Game Boy—2 hours	Loss of Xbox—rest of the day
No dessert or treat	Monetary fine
No use of phone	Small chore—wash bathroom sink
Larger chore—weed yard	Write a paragraph
No conversation—15 minutes	Removal of DVD, iPod
No friend over	Reduced computer time

Groundings, fines, chores and losses like these can be very useful as consequences, and there are many other options. The list of time-out alternatives is limited only by your imagination. Remember to keep the punishments fair and reasonable; your goal is to teach the child something, not to be cruel or get revenge.

Consequences can also be what some people call logical or natural, which means the punishment fits the misbehavior. A child's hitting 3, for example, might mean the end of a pleasant shopping trip. Or a count of 3 might mean the loss of an ice cream bar that was dripping on the car seat. The TV can be turned off if warnings to turn the volume down are ignored. Remember when applying natural consequences that kids are still just kids. Exasperated lectures from you along the lines of "Well, this wouldn't have happened if you'd have simply listened to me in the first place" are unnecessary. Your chattering also interferes with your child's ability to appreciate the connection between his behavior and its consequences.

You can use counting for lots of things:

Tantrums   **Disrespect**

Sibling Rivalry

Plus lots more! Whining, arguing, yelling,
teasing, throwing the football in the house, and
a whole host of other obnoxious behaviors.

6
Frequently Asked Questions

Be prepared for a few surprises.

1-2-3 *Magic's* counting strategy is straightforward, but managing kids' irritating behavior is never an easy job. At this point you probably have a number of questions about this first big phase of parenting. Let's take a look at some of the most frequently asked ones.

1. What if the child won't go to time-out?

If the child won't go to his room after hitting a count of 3, remember you are not allowed to use little adult attempts at persuasion, such as, "Come on now, do what Dad told you. It's only for five minutes and then you'll be able to go back and play. I'm not asking a lot ... etc., etc." What you do instead depends on how big you are and how big the child is.

The little kids. Let's say you weigh 125 pounds, and your five-year-old son weighs forty-five pounds. If he doesn't go to his room at 3, you simply move toward him. Some kids will then stay two feet ahead of you all the way to the room. That's OK; they'll soon start going by themselves. Other kids, though, have to be "escorted" (keep your mouth closed while doing this), which can mean taking them gently by the arm, as well as dragging or carrying them—kicking and screaming (that's them kicking and screaming, not you)—to the room. No hitting or spanking. That's if you're 125 pounds and they're forty-five.

The bigger kids. Now let's imagine that it's five years later. Your ten-year-old son at this point weighs ninety-five pounds, and you—through a rigid program of diet and exercise—still weigh 125. You are no longer in a position to get into anything physical with this boy. He's too big, and wrestling matches make a fool out of you.

Your savior here will be the time-out alternative. If after your "That's 3, take 10," the young lad doesn't appear to be going anywhere, you inform him that he has a choice. He can go for time-out, or choose one of the following: bedtime will be one-half-hour earlier, fifty cents will come off his allowance, or he can forgo any electronic (including battery-operated) entertainment for the evening. "Community service" is also a nice option—some kind of small chore (some parents have used weeding or scrubbing a sink or toilet). Many parents let the child pick the consequence. If the child refuses, the parent selects the punishment.

Quik Tip

What if the child won't go to time-out? With the little kids, it's OK to "escort" them to the chair or room. That could mean carry them, but you must keep quiet! With the older kids, you will switch to a time-out alternative. Give them a choice or decide yourself, then walk away.

A problem arises here, however, because your child hasn't gone to his room and the two of you are still face to face. Lots of kids in this situation want to stick around and argue with you about how stupid your rules are, how stupid *1-2-3 Magic* is, and how stupid the guy who wrote it must have been.

You know you're not allowed to argue. What are you going to do? You can use a "reverse time-out," in which *you* just turn around and leave the room. Go to your room or even the bathroom if necessary, stock them with good reading materials beforehand, and wait the storm out. Or walk around the house a few times. But don't talk.

Some parents have asked, "Why should I be the one to leave? After all, I'm the adult." Fine. Stay put if you can keep quiet and avoid both being provocative and being provoked. But if your real motive is the desire to stick around for a good fight, that's a bad strategy.

2. Can you count different misbehaviors to get to three?

Yes. You don't have to have different counts for each different kind of misbehavior. Imagine: "Let's see, he's on a 1 for throwing that block across the room. He's on a 2 for teasing his sister. He's on a 1 for yelling at me. He's on a 2 for ..."

This routine would soon drive you insane and you'd need a personal computer to keep track of everything. So if the child pushes his sister, for example, "That's 1"; throws a block across the room, "That's 2"; and then screams at you for counting him, "That's 3, take 5." The child is gone.

Mom could say "1," Dad could say "2" and Mom or Dad could say, "That's 3." In fact, we encourage you to share the joy. Actually, it's better if Mom and Dad *do* both count, because then the kids know that both parents are behind the plan—they are consistent and really serious. The involvement of both parents makes it easier for the children to shape up. In the same way, the involvement of both home and school in doing the 1-2-3 also makes it easier for kids to behave—especially the really difficult children.

3. Can you ever ignore anything? Introducing the MBA!

How do you know when you should count? Usually it's not too difficult to tell. Most of the time, if you're irritated about something and that something is a Stop behavior, you should be counting. Just to be sure, you and your kids can write a list of countable behaviors.

However, there can be times when you're irritated but the kids are not really misbehaving and you should not count. We call these activities "MBAs," Minor But Aggravating actions that may rub you the wrong way but are not really misbehavior. Humming, singing the same song over and over, rolling the eyes and stomping to time-out, squirminess, chasing the dog and eating all the frosting off the top of the cupcake first may be examples. If the child's not really misbehaving and you're in a bad mood, the best thing to do is grit your teeth and keep quiet.

The question of ignoring certain types of behavior leaves room for some variation among parents. Why? Because some parents simply have longer fuses than others. Some parents, for example, will ignore kids' rolling their eyes, stomping off, grumbling and whining, while other parents will count. Some parents will ignore a child's yelling or even pounding walls as long as he's on his way to time-out. Other parents will lengthen the rest period for that kind of behavior. Either strategy is correct if it is done consistently. You have to clearly define what kinds of child behavior, in your well-considered opinion, are too obnoxious, too rude, too aggressive or too dangerous. Then make up your mind that those behaviors are the ones that will be counted.

CAUTION

Your kids already have their MBAs! Minor But Aggravating actions that may rub you the wrong way but which are not really misbehavior. These may include humming, squirminess, rolling the eyes, and eating the frosting of the top of the cupcake first.

But in the beginning with *1-2-3 Magic*, don't ignore genuine misbehavior. In the beginning, when in doubt, count! After a while, when you're getting a good response at 1 or 2, you may be able to let up a little.

Let's say, for example, that after a few weeks getting used to the 1-2-3 program, your child does something right in front of you that would normally be counted. Instead of counting right away, just watch your youngster. The child can almost "feel" the count coming. Sometimes, if you say nothing, the child will spontaneously exercise self-control and stop the misbehavior. This response is ideal, because now the child is internalizing the rules and controlling himself without direct parental intervention. Isn't that the kind of person you want to drop off at the dorm on the first day of his freshman year in college?

4. How long do you take in between counts?

About five seconds. Just long enough to allow the child time to shape up. Remember that we're counting Stop (obnoxious) behaviors, such as arguing, whining, badgering and teasing, and for obnoxious behavior it only takes a child one second to cooperate with you by stopping the annoying activity. We certainly don't want to give a child half an hour to continue a tantrum before giving him a 2.

Counting is perfectly designed to produce the one second's worth of motivation necessary for cooperation. We give the kids five seconds, though, which is a little more generous. Why five seconds? Because this brief pause gives the youngsters time to think things over and do the right thing. In those few seconds—provided the adult keeps quiet—kids learn to take responsibility for their own behavior.

5. If a child hits a 1 or a 2, does he stay at that count for the rest of the day, even if he does nothing else wrong?

No. The time perspective of young children is short. You would not say "That's 1" at nine in the morning, "That's 2" at 11:15, and "That's 3, take 5" at three in the afternoon. So we have what we call our "window of opportunity" rule: If a six-year-old, for example, does three things wrong in a thirty-minute period, each warning counts toward the total of three. But if he does one thing wrong, then an hour goes by, then he does something else he shouldn't, you can start back at 1.

Very few children manipulate this rule by doing one thing, allowing thirty minutes to pass, and then figuring, "Now I get a free one!" If you feel a youngster is trying to get away with this, simply make the next count a 2 instead of going back to 1.

The window of opportunity should be longer as kids get older. Here is a general guideline: For four-year olds consider a time period of ten or fifteen minutes; for eleven-year olds think about two to three hours. Classroom teachers in the primary grades do not usually use a short window because, with twenty-five children in your class, this would allow for too much potential misbehavior in too short a period of time. Instead, the counting period in school is expanded to cover the entire morning, all counts are washed away at lunchtime, then the afternoon is treated as a new and separate window.

6. Can you use a time-out chair instead of a room?

You can use a stair or a chair for a time-out (don't use a corner of the room), but only if the child does not make a game out of the situation. Some kids, for example, sit on the chair at first, but then start gradually losing contact with it. Eventually they may just be touching their little finger to the chair and looking at you like, "What are you going to do about this?" If your rule for time-out is simply that the child must stay in contact with the chair, this is no problem. But if the child is getting on and off or away from the chair and you're uncertain what to do, this kind of game will ruin the discipline.

We usually prefer that visual contact between parent and child be broken during the rest period, so the child can't tease or provoke you. That's why the child's bedroom or other safe room is preferable. Many parents, however, have successfully used stairs and chairs and many report that the kids—even some wild ones!—sit still on them, don't talk and don't keep getting off. As a matter of fact, parents are often very creative in coming up with places for time-outs.

7. What if the child won't stay in his room?

Many kids will stay in the room for the time-out, even if the door isn't shut (it doesn't have to be shut). Others, however, will keep coming out. With very small children, one alternative is to just stand there blocking the way or to hold the door shut. After a few time-outs the kids get the idea that they can't come out. This tactic won't work, however, if you keep getting into major tugs of war with the door. If your discipline comes down to this level, you look stupid.

A second alternative is to block the child's exit with the kind of gate that squeezes against the door jambs. These gates can be used as long as the children are not able to either climb over or knock down the device. Yet another option is to start the time-out over if the child comes out prematurely. Some parents will then double the time of the second rest period. This method, of course, won't be much help with two- or three-year-olds because they won't understand, but with older children it can work well. Explain once and then start.

Some kids, however, are so rambunctious that they just keep coming out and accumulate what seem like thousands of extra time-out minutes. What should you do? You need to secure the door in some way or another. There are several options.

Some parents of difficult children, believe it or not, have made the child's bedroom door into a "Dutch" door. They saw the door in half, then lock the bottom part and leave the top part open during the time-out. You may think that's a pretty drastic solution. It is, but some kids require drastic (but gentle) solutions.

Also available are plastic door knob covers. These devices cover the knob and have to be squeezed tightly enough to be able to turn the knob and open the door. Many young children aren't strong enough to accomplish this.

Another idea is to simply put some kind of lock on the door. This advice worries some parents who think that their child will become claustrophobic or that locking the door is abusive. Locking the door for a short period of time is not by itself abusive, but for some groups (e.g., foster parents) and in some places (e.g., some provinces of Canada) it is illegal. If you have a really difficult child, you should check into what regulations hold for your situation and get some professional advice.

Here's an option for locking the door. You tell your child that as long as he stays in his room, the door will remain open or simply shut. But the first time he comes out, the door gets locked for the rest period. Many children will quickly learn to stay put without the door having to be locked. If you still prefer gates to locks, purchase one of the more solid gates that bolts into the door jambs. If the child can climb over the gate, get a taller one or put two up.

Key Concept

The main point is this: It is totally unproductive and harmful to be chasing the kids back into the room all the time. The child needs to know that there is a barrier that she is stuck with for a short period of time.

The main point is this: Some children, including many of our ADHD friends, will try to keep coming out of the room. Securing the door in some way or another is absolutely essential. It is totally unproductive and harmful to be chasing the kids back in the room all the time; the child must know that the door is a barrier that he's stuck with for a short time. Once children learn they can't get out of the room, they will stop tantruming and calmly accept the brief period of quiet.

If you worry about the safety of the child, childproof the room, secure any windows and remain outside the door during the time-out, but try not to let the child know you're there. If you still feel the youngster is not safe alone in the room or if you feel he would suffer excessive separation anxiety, you may go in the room during the time-out. But no eye contact and no talking!

And don't forget the one-minute-per-year rule for the length of the rest period. Remember that you may not increase the length of the time-out simply because you're in a bad mood. You can increase the length of time-out—to a point—if the child did something that is exceptionally bad.

8. What do you do if the child counts you back?!

Your five-year-old is whining at you because you wouldn't take her to the pool on a hot summer day. You look at her, hold up one finger, and say, "That's 1." She looks back at you, holds up one tiny finger, and says, "That's 1 to you, too!"

What should you do? Oddly enough, this common occurrence sometimes throws even the most confident parents for a loop. They are at a loss how to handle the unexpected rebellion. Some parents have even said, "*1-2-3 Magic* doesn't work—the kid just counts me back!"

So what do you do? Your kids do not have the authority to count anyone (unless you give that power to them). The child might as well have said, "The moon is made of cream cheese." The comment itself means nothing—but it might be a countable misbehavior.

Here's how you decide. If the child's remark appears to be a humorous attempt to tease you a little, you can just ignore it. If her "That's 1 to you, too!" however, is sarcastic and disrespectful, count it by simply holding up two fingers and saying nothing. If the child again mocks your response, she will have just arrived at 3. Repeat when necessary.

Can one of your kids count another one? Generally no. The only time this can occur is if one child is old enough to babysit the other. But make sure to get a report when you come back.

9. Does the room have to be a sterile environment?

No. Many books tell you the time-out room should be modeled after a cell in a state penitentiary. Complete and utter boredom—that'll teach 'em! This is unnecessary. The child can go to the room and read, take a nap, play with Legos, draw and so on. She doesn't even have to stay on her bed. Just to be safe, though, there are three things that are forbidden: no phone, no friends and no electronic entertainment.

Some people ask: "Well then, just how is a rest period supposed to work? My kid tells me that time-out's fine with her—she doesn't care and she'll just go upstairs and play." Don't pay much attention to any child who says, "I don't care." That comment usually means the opposite: She does care. And if her room were such a great place to be, she would have already been up there.

The fact of the matter is, the power of the 1-2-3 does not come so much from the time-out itself; it usually comes from the interruption of the child's activities. It just so happens that when this girl was timed out for hitting her brother, she was watching her favorite TV show. Now she has to miss a big chunk of the show. No one—including you—likes to be interrupted and miss out on something fun.

If you really feel the time-out is not effective, consider three things. First, are you still talking too much and getting too emotional during discipline efforts? Parental outbursts ruin everything. Second, if you feel you are remaining calm and time-out is still not working, consider another time-out place or room. Third, consider time-out alternatives.

10. Why three counts? Children should respond the first time you ask! Why give the kids three chances to misbehave?

1-2-3 Magic is an interesting phenomenon. Some people think counting is too dictatorial, while others see counting as a sign of parental weakness.

The reason for three counts is simple: you want to give the kids two chances—the first two counts—to shape up (unless what they did was so serious that it merited an automatic 3). How are children going to learn to do the right thing if they never get a chance? And with counting, the "chance" comes right away—in the first few seconds following the count. That immediate opportunity helps them learn. They're just kids!

11. What if you have other people over?

By this time, you can probably anticipate the answer to this question. You will need to 1) get used to counting in front of other people and 2) not alter your strategy one bit when others are watching. The ultimate test, of course, is when you're out in public (see next chapter). For right now, we'll discuss what should happen in the safety of your own home.

From time to time, other people will be at your home when your kids decide to act up. In fact, the presence of other people often seems to trigger disruptive behavior in many kids, presenting parents with a complicated challenge: disciplining children while on stage. Among the groups of people who perversely decide to put you in this awkward position are other kids, other parents (with or without their kids), and finally, grandparents. Let's examine the problems presented by each group.

Other kids. If your youngster has a friend over, count your child just as you would if no one else were there. If your child gets timed out, he goes to the room and—remember—his friend may not join him. Just explain to the other boy or girl that you're using this new system and his buddy will be back in five minutes or so. If your son or daughter says to you, as some have, "Mom, it's so embarrassing when you count me in front of my friends," you say to them once, "If you don't want to be embarrassed, you can behave."

Quik Tip
If your youngster looks at you and says, "It's so embarrassing when you count me in front of my friends!" you simply reply, "If you don't want to be embarrassed, you can behave."

Another thing you can do in this situation is count the other child, too. After all, it's your house. If his parent is there, though, you'd better ask permission and explain a bit before you go disciplining her child.

Another variation with other kids over is "1-2-3, 1-2-3, 1-2-3: out of the house to play." This can be very helpful, especially if you have a difficult child who often gets overly excited when a playmate is over. With this routine, at the third time-out, instead of sending your child to the room again, both kids must now leave the house for a specified time (assuming the weather isn't nasty) and play outside. This variation of the 1-2-3 is very popular in southern California.

Or—even better—1-2-3, 1-2-3, 1-2-3, then send them over to the other kid's house to play. I've done it!

Other adults. If you have other adults over at your home, you will probably feel considerably more nervous counting your child. This discomfort is normal. Although you may feel a little self-conscious at first, you'll soon get used to doing the 1-2-3 under these circumstances. So count! If you don't take the plunge, your children will sense that you are much easier prey when other people are around.

On the other hand, when you count in front of another parent, something surprising may happen that you will enjoy. You're talking to a friend and your child rudely and loudly interrupts you demanding a snack. You calmly say, "That's 1." Your child not only quiets down, she also leaves the room. The other parent looks at you like, "What did you do?!" Just tell her about the 1-2-3 and explain how it works. This scene is one of the major ways that *1-2-3 Magic* gets passed around.

Grandparents. For our purposes here, there are three types of grandparents, whether you're visiting them or they're visiting you. The first—and rarest—type of grandparent is the *cooperative* grandparent. She will count along with you. You say 1, Grandma says 2, and so on. That kind of cooperation is super, but it doesn't happen as much as we'd like.

Like the first type, the second type of grandparent is also nice to have around. This person we call the *passive* or *unintrusive* grandparent. This grandma or grandpa leaves you alone when you're disciplining the kids and doesn't interfere. That's often not easy for a grandparent.

The third type of grandparent, however, is the *antagonistic* grandparent. He will say something to you like this: "You have to read a book to learn how to raise your kids?! Why, when I was a boy, all Dad had to do was look at his belt." You know the rest. The message is that you don't need any of this modern, psychological stuff.

A second kind of antagonistic grandparent will actually interfere with your discipline. You say to little Bobby, "That's 3, take 5," and before he can move, Grandma butts in and says, "Oh, little Bobby didn't really do anything. Bobby, come and sit on Grandma's lap for a while."

Some parents ask at this point: "Can you count the grandparents?" Probably not, but you do have an assertiveness problem on your hands. You may have to say something like, "You know, Mom, I love you very much, but these are our kids and this is the way we're raising them. If you can't go along with the agenda, the visit may have to be cut short a little." Although this statement will be a very difficult one to make, the comment will definitely be an investment in your children's future.

Can you imagine saying that to your parents?!

12. What if the child won't come out from time-out?

You probably know the answer to this one: Relax and enjoy yourself! You go to the bedroom door and say, "Time's up." Your son or daughter replies, "I'm never coming out again as long as I live!" Don't say, "Good!" or anything like that. Just walk away—never chase a martyr.

On the other hand, do not cheat by extending the time-out. Imagine your child's time-out was for five minutes. You just noticed, though, that you got distracted and eight minutes elapsed. You think, "Oh, it's so peaceful! And she's being so quiet in her room! Why let her out?" Wrong—no fair. Keep an eye on the clock or timer, then tell the child when the time is up. If your girl has fallen asleep—and if it's OK for her to nap at this time of day—let her snooze for a bit.

Some kids always want a hug and some reassurance when time out is over. What do you do? Give them a hug! But be careful with these little huggers. If a child repeatedly requests a hug, you'd better check to make sure you're doing the 1-2-3 correctly. Some kids, of course, are just very sensitive and any kind of discipline upsets them a little. Other children, however, need reassurance because you were too harsh— emotionally or physically—before you sent them to the room. So if you get a little hugger, make sure you're gently following the No-Talking and No-Emotion rules.

13. Help—my kids go nuts when I'm on the phone!!

This problem brings back vivid memories to all parents. It seems that there are no parents in the entire world whose children don't act up when the parents are on the phone. The ringing seems to be the signal that it's time to cut loose!

At our house, the dog would also get into the act. The phone would ring and the dog would bark. The dog's bark was a signal to the kids, "We've got another victim on the line, get down here and let's torture him for a while!" Then they'd all be running around, yelling and barking and having a wonderful time. Whoever was on the phone, though, would feel trapped and frustrated.

Why does it seem that children always act up when you're on the phone? At first I thought it was because the kids were jealous because their parent was talking to someone else and ignoring them. There may be some of this feeling, but now I believe the main reason is that the youngsters think you are *helpless*. The kids seem to believe that since your head is attached to the phone, you won't be able to do anything to counter their raising a ruckus.

What you do is count the children just as you would if you weren't on the phone—much like when you have other people over. While you're on the phone you have somebody else present—but only listening, not watching. You may have to interrupt your conversation to count. You may have to put the phone down or explain what you're doing to the person you're talking to, or even hang up so you can escort a little one to her room. Long distance calls become more expensive, but whatever it takes, do it. Otherwise the children will know that you are a sitting duck every time someone calls.

Quik Tip

Why do kids always seem to act up whenever you're on the phone or on your Blackberry? It's probably because they think you are helpless. Let them know you're not by counting just as you would if you weren't talking to anyone.

This phone routine is not easy in the beginning. After a while, though, many parents succeed in training the children to the point where the adults don't have to say anything while counting. They simply hold up the appropriate number of fingers while they continue their conversation! And the children respond because they know Mom or Dad means business. If you have gotten to this point, it's a mighty handy tactic to use when you're talking on the telephone.

14. What if the kid wrecks the room during his so-called "rest period"?

By far, the vast majority of children will not be room-wreckers. Only a small percentage of kids will throw things around and mess up the room. An even smaller percentage of children will break things, tear their beds apart or kick holes in the wall. These kids do exist, however, and their parents need to know how to handle these sometimes scary actions.

The whole point behind *1-2-3 Magic* is that parents be ready for anything, rather than feeling defensive and worrying, "Oh no, what is he going to do now?" We want your attitude and message to the children to be something like this: "You're my child and I'm your parent. I love you, and it's my job to train and discipline you. I don't expect you to be perfect, and when you do something wrong, this is what I will do."

Key Concept

The point behind *1-2-3 Magic* is that parents be ready for anything, rather than worrying what the kids are going to do next. The message is: "I love you and it's my job to train and discipline you. I don't expect you to be perfect, and when you act up, this is what I will do."

The credit for the solution to the room-wrecking problem comes from a couple who visited my office a long time ago. They had an eight-year-old boy who was very nice to me in my office, but—according to his Mom and Dad—was "hell on wheels" everywhere else. These parents said they were thinking of putting this boy's name on their mail box, because it felt like he was running the house. They often referred to their son as "King Louis XIV."

This behavior obviously couldn't go on, so I asked these parents if they wanted to learn *1-2-3 Magic*. They said yes. I taught them the program, prepared them for testing and manipulation and they went home to get started. This boy had been used to running the house—but when his parents got home they were ready for him.

When King Louis hit 3 for the first time, he could not believe what happened. How his parents got him to his room for his first "rest period" is still a mystery, but when he got there, he totally—and I mean totally—trashed the place. His first tactic, and perhaps the favorite of all room-wreckers—was to empty his dresser and throw his clothes all over the floor. Then he ripped the blankets and sheets off his bed. Next he pushed the mattress and box springs off the bed frame. Then he proceeded to his closet, took out all his hanging clothes, and one by one threw them all over the room. After that, all his toys were flung out of the closet. Finally, he went to the window and tore down his curtains.

What did his parents do? Amazingly, they didn't call me for help. The first thing they did was nothing! They didn't clean up the mess or have King Louis clean it up. Any cleaning up would have meant loading the boy's gun again for the next time-out: another perfectly neat room to wreck. Second, Mom and Dad continued to count their son aggressively but fairly. When the young lad earned a 3, he got a 3 and a consequence. No fudging around with fractions such as, "That's 2-and-a-half, that's

2-and-three-quarters." The parents would hit him with his well-earned 3 and then send him to his bedroom to rearrange the trash. When bedtime came, this boy had to find his pajamas. He also had to find his bed. In the mornings, his clothes for school didn't match for a week.

How long did it take for King Louis to learn that there was new management in the old *maison*? It took about ten days for him to start calming down during time-out. Then, after three or four days of peaceful time-outs, his parents helped him clean up his room. After that—believe it or not—he hated to be counted, and his parents would stop him on a dime with a count of 1.

Now, did we break this boy's spirit? Was he now going to be an eternal marshmallow for the rest of his life? Certainly not. Now he was really and consistently the nice kid I had seen in the office, and his parents were in charge of their own house as they should have been. In addition, the boy started behaving better in school, where the teacher was also using the 1-2-3.

If you think you are going to have a room-wrecker, before starting the 1-2-3 check out two things. If there is anything dangerous or harmful in the room, or anything valuable that can be broken, take it out before the first "rest period." For example, if the child has a hammer and a saw in the room, or if Grandma has her Hummel collection on top of his dresser, get those out of there before you start counting.

15. Room-wrecking is one thing, but what do you do if your child urinates on the floor during time-out?

Some kids have done it—usually preschoolers. You send them to time-out and they are so mad, they pull down their pants and cut loose. What do you do? You time them out to the bathroom.

I know what you're thinking: "How naive! Do you really expect the youngster to use the facilities appropriately?" The answer is "No, we don't expect the youngster to use the facilities appropriately." That's not the point. The point is this: What's easier to clean, the bedroom rug or the bathroom floor? If the child goes on the bedroom rug, cleaning is an expensive project. If the child goes on the bathroom floor or the smaller bathroom rug, it's a different story.

The same advice holds true if you have one of these children who can get himself so upset that he throws up. In every workshop I've ever done, there are a few parents who have kids like this. Make sure the bathroom's safe, then time him out to the bathroom. And stay cool!

16. While we're on the subject, can you use counting for toilet training?

No. Counting is not especially effective for potty training. One reason is that if you are trying to count children's messing their pants, you don't always know the exact moment when the "accident" occurs, and so you don't know just when to count. In addition, most experts agree that punishing kids for wetting or soiling is not particularly helpful.

Though there are several effective ways to get kids to go on the toilet, my favorite method is for the parent to do very little formal training. Too many parents are in too big a hurry to get their kids potty trained, and this big rush can cause all kinds of trouble. Instead, let the kids see you use the toilet and get them a potty chair of their own. Most children will eventually learn how to use the thing without much direct coaching from you. When they are successful, you can then praise and reward them.

Another frequently unsuccessful parent tactic in this regard is repeatedly asking a child—when he's looking squirmy—if he has to go to the bathroom. It's much better to say this: "Some day you're gonna surprise me and go on the potty!"

17. What if there's an obvious problem between the children, but you didn't see what happened?

Your daughter, Suzie, comes running into the kitchen and yells, "Dad, Bobby should get a 1!" You haven't the slightest idea what the problem is, but the chances are the issue revolves around sibling rivalry. In general our rule is this: If you didn't see the argument or conflict, you don't count it; if you hear it, you can count it.

If you're in the kitchen and you hear a ruckus starting in the family room, for example, there's nothing to stop you from calling, "Hey guys, that's 1." Of course, you want to use this rule with flexibility. If you feel one child is consistently being victimized by another, you may have to intervene and count just the aggressive child. On the other hand, if the tattling is getting out of hand, many parents decide to count the tattler.

18. Does being counted hurt the child's self-esteem?

Most kids aren't counted a lot, so the mere quantity of counts is usually not a problem. Once you've gotten started at home, many children will not get any counts for days at a time. In a regular education classroom, on an average day, fewer than five children will get any count at all.

For those children who do get counted more often, if you are doing the 1-2-3 correctly, there should be no significant threat of hurting self-esteem. What *will* hurt youngsters' self-esteem is all the yelling, arguing, name-calling, sarcasm or hitting you may do if you don't control yourself. In addition, as you will see later, your feedback to your children should be much more positive than negative. And one count is a bit of negative feedback. Therefore, you will want to more than balance off your occasional counting with other activities or strategies, such as affection, shared fun, listening and praise.

19. Should you ever spank a child?

It's about time that people face up to reality: *the vast majority of spankings are parental temper tantrums*. They are in no way attempts to train or educate a child. They are simply the angry outbursts of a parent who has lost control, doesn't know what to do and wants revenge by inflicting pain. Parents who have big problems with self-control and anger management try to justify and rationalize spanking by saying things like, "You have to set limits," "It's for their own good," and "Having to hit the kids hurts me more than it does them."

It's true there are cultures and groups where spanking is perceived as a legitimate discipline technique. There are also some people who really do see—and use—spanking as a training device. But research suggests that *excessive* physical discipline tends to generate anxiety in children, lower their self-esteem and make the kids more likely to become aggressive themselves.

Generally speaking, though, adults who spank do not care one bit about research. I have on occasion talked till I'm blue in the face with parents like these, and, sadly enough, changing their opinions and their discipline habits is often a lost cause. Remember, the whole point of the 1-2-3 program is to avoid the Talk-Persuade-Argue-Yell-Hit routine.

20. My child has a fit when I try to drop him off at preschool. No matter how much I try to reassure him, he screams whenever I try to leave.

Though separation anxiety is normal in little children, the kids' desperate screams when you try to leave them at preschool, with a sitter or even at grandma's can be very upsetting to you. Here's what you do. Bite your upper lip and become the Master of the Quick Exit. When dropping children off (or leaving home), kiss the kids goodbye, tell them when you'll see them again and get out of there! The longer you stay and the more you talk, the worse you will make everything.

If these awful moments make you feel like a totally cold and uncaring adult, call back later and ask whoever the caretaker is how long your child cried. The average is eighty seconds.

21. Shouldn't the kids ever apologize?

This is a tough question. If you're currently asking the kids to apologize, and that routine is working well, fine. Keep in mind, however, that many apologies are really exercises in hypocrisy. Requiring an apology is often simply part of the child's punishment—not a learning experience involving sorrow or compassion.

For example, your two sons have gotten into a fight. You break up the tussle, then demand that they apologize to one another. The older boy glares at the younger, and with a sneer on his face says, "I'm sorry." His tone is forced, begrudging and sarcastic.

Now let me ask you two questions about this child's response. First, was this a real apology? Of course not. His comment was merely a continuation of the original battle, but on a verbal level. Second, was his statement a lie? The answer is yes. If you want to insist on apologies, make sure that you are not simply asking your children to lie.

22. What if my boy or girl misbehaves at school?

The first time this happens, ask your child to explain. Don't "double punish" the youngster if the teacher already took some disciplinary action. Depending on the severity of the incident, you may want to talk to the teacher. Some problems will vanish without a lot of effort.

The second time a school misbehavior occurs, you will want to talk to the teacher. You may even want to talk to the teacher with your child. Though you may still decide to not take action, if the behavior continues you will want to work out a daily or weekly behavior chart (see charting in Chapter 13) that the teacher fills out and sends home to keep you up to date. You may decide to hook up this chart with both rewards and consequences that you administer at home. If this intervention doesn't succeed after a few weeks, try modifying your rewards, consequences or chart itself. If that doesn't work after a few more weeks, consider a professional evaluation through the school or privately.

CAUTION
Poor grades are not really a misbehavior. And punishment for poor grades is a strategy that is way more often unsuccessful than useful. Try a friendly reward system first, and if that doesn't work, consider a professional evaluation.

One note of caution: poor grades are not really a misbehavior. And punishment-only methods for dealing with poor grades usually fail. Instead, use the charting-and-if-that-fails-evaluation system described above.

23. What about the 1-2-3 and special needs kids?

1-2-3 Magic can be used with typically developing kids or special needs kids, such as children with ADHD, learning disabilities, Oppositional Defiant Disorder, depression and even autistic spectrum disorders. The main thing is that the child have a mental age of about two.

Usually the counting method doesn't require much modification, but two special instances, both involving anxiety, should be mentioned. First, some children seem to become more anxious (not angry, but anxious) when they are verbally counted. Sometimes using a visual stimulus such as three cards (green = 1, yellow = 2, red = 3) is helpful.

Second, it often is not helpful to count anxiety. Anxiety, after all, is not a willful misbehavior. A child who screams at the sight of a mosquito or who bellows furiously when you try to leave her at school will be better handled with reassurance and gentle but firm structure. See the Appendix for more references.

24. When should you talk?

By now you know that during a discipline episode is not a good time to talk. This is not what they call a "teachable moment." There are better times to impart wisdom (see Chapter 21).

25. I like the program. How do I get my husband involved?

Husbands are sometimes difficult to get on board when it comes to systematic parenting programs. Here's what you do. Get a copy of the first (blue) DVD, *1-2-3 Magic: Managing Difficult Behavior.* This covers the program through approximately Chapter 12 of this book, and it's often available at your library. Ask your husband to watch it. But there's a catch. You can't be in the room with him, because you may have a tendency to say, "See, this is what you need to be doing." That will turn him off for sure. After he watches the DVD, if he's willing to cooperate, get started and add parenting jobs 2 and 3 later (purple DVD, *More 1-2-3 Magic*, or Chapters 13-24 of this book). Using *1-2-3 Magic* with the kids is good for marriages!

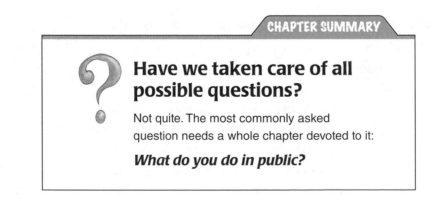

CHAPTER SUMMARY

Have we taken care of all possible questions?

Not quite. The most commonly asked question needs a whole chapter devoted to it:

What do you do in public?

7

Out in Public

Did you ever feel like crawling into a hole?

We now must come to grips with the worst nightmare of every parent: what to do in public. No one wants to look like a child abuser in aisle 5, the candy aisle, of the local grocery store. And kids—even very young toddlers—seem to have automatic radar that can sense psychological vulnerability in anxious parents.

Once they have learned the mechanics of the 1-2-3, many parents worry about being out in public where there is no time-out room. Believe it or not, this problem can be solved without too much difficulty. That, my fellow parents, happens to be the good news. The bad news is that there is a worse problem lurking in the shadows, and deep in her heart every parent knows what that problem is.

Your biggest problem in public is that your little ones can hold something over your head that they can't hold over your head in private: the *threat of public embarrassment*. This fear of embarrassment and public disapproval has at times made even the most competent parents forget what they're supposed to do, abandon tactics and crumble. Try to remember this basic principle: The long-term welfare of your kids comes before short-term worries about what others are going to think of you.

Counting in Public

Let's imagine that you do have a five-year-old and that yes, in fact, aisle 5 in the grocery store, the candy aisle, is one of your biggest problems. It seems as though every time you go down that aisle, your son asks for candy, you say no because all the candy bars are huge, and then the little boy proceeds to throw a ferocious tantrum. He throws himself on the floor, screams at the top of his lungs and—don't you love this part?—a crowd has gathered to see how you're going to handle the crisis.

What do you do? The first thing you do is make sure you have the 1-2-3 rolling fairly well at home. "Fairly well" means you are getting a good response at 1 or 2 most of the time. Why not all the time? Because he's just a kid.

Now you're in aisle 5, your son is howling, and the audience has as-sembled. You look down at the unhappy little monster, hold up one finger and say, "That's 1." You say this as calmly and as firmly as you would at home. What is the key here? The key is not so much what you say as what you don't say. You do not, for example, let yourself be intimidated by the threat of public embarrassment and whisper, "Come on now, I don't want you making a fool of me in front of all these people." You do that and the child will *know* that you can be had for a nickel; he won't need the candy bar because he's about to have more fun with you.

Proceed to 2 and then to 3, if necessary. Do not look at anyone else other than your child. At this point, of course, parents wonder, "What are we going to do at 3? There's no time-out room." This problem is easier to solve than you think.

Time-Out Room, Time-Out Place

Over the many years of developing the *1-2-3 Magic* program, parents taught me what to do in situations like this. These were parents who, in the heat of battle, had to come up with rest-period solutions while in the restaurants, in the theaters, in stores, at the museum, at the ballpark and in church.

We call the solution, "Time-Out Room, Time-Out Place." There is always either a room, something like a room, or a symbolic place where a time-out can be served. For example, in the aisle 5 conflict we just described, at 3 some parents will just stay right where they are and hold the child's hand for several minutes. The adult says nothing during this period. That's a time-out place. One young mother actually carried a small time-out mat around with her, and she would simply plop it onto the floor of the store when necessary. Other parents have put little children in the grocery cart for the consequence. That's almost a time-out room.

Other ideas include a corner of the store—a time-out place. For more rambunctious children, the bathroom of the store can serve the same purpose. Let them scream their heads off in there for a while. Some parents, feeling their children play up to an audience, will actually leave the grocery cart right where it is and take the child back to the car to do the rest period. That's like a time-out room.

Using the car like this makes some people ask, "Why should I have to go through all the trouble of leaving the store?" The answer is because 1) they're just kids, 2) they're still learning how to behave and 3) "all that trouble" is a sound investment in their future and your peace of mind.

Here's another idea. If the child is old enough and you won't worry about him, at 3 have him wait for you—perhaps next to one of the cash registers or next to the information booth—till you're done shopping. Don't do this unless you're sure the child will be safe.

> **Quik Tip**
> When you're out in public, there is always either a room, something like a room, or a symbolic location where a time-out can be served. And don't forget your time-out alternatives. Just because people are watching does not mean that you have to be at your kids' mercy!

During any time-out, you do not talk to the child. No lecturing, screaming or nagging. Keeping quiet is often very hard, but after a while the youngsters get the idea you mean business. And yes, there have been parents who felt the fuss was bad enough that they left a half-full grocery cart and went back home.

If the Kids Don't Want to Go

Imagine this situation. You're cooking a new recipe for dinner and you are so excited about this new dish that you can hardly stand it.

At 5:15 p.m., however, you suddenly realize you are missing two essential ingredients. To make matters worse, your six-year-old and eight-year-old are in the other room playing well together for the first time in two-and-a-half years. You're going to have to interrupt them and there's no time to get a sitter. You know they don't want to go.

Here's what you do. Tell the kids that you have to go shopping, it will take about an hour and they have to go with you. You know they don't want to, but you're stuck. Tell them the deal will be this: If they're "good" while you're out (meaning they don't hit a count of 4—you're giving them an extra count because of the length of the trip and because they don't want to go), you'll buy them a treat. Their reward will be $1 cash or $1 worth of whatever else they may want to buy (adjust figures for inflation!). If they hit the count of 4 during the trip, however, the reward is gone.

Some parents feel this is bribery. It is! But the real definition of bribery is paying someone to do something illegal. Here we're paying the kids to do something legal, and it works.

If the Kids Do Want to Go

My wife and I had a very interesting experience using a TOA tactic with our kids when we initially tried going out for ice cream in the evening. The first few times we went out for our after-dinner treat, the kids fought like cats and dogs in the back seat. By the time we all got our ice cream, no one was in any kind of a party mood anymore.

So finally one evening I told the kids this: "Guys, we're going out for ice cream. But there's going to be a new deal. If you guys hit a count of 3 before we get to the store, we turn right around and come home. Nobody will get any ice cream."

With hopeful hearts, we took off in the car. The children started fighting. I said, "That's 1, third count blows the trip." Sure enough, they were soon at 2, and then, only half way to the ice cream store, they hit a 3. I turned the car around and went home. The TOA was the outing ending. The kids were not pleased; they looked stunned and resentful.

A few days later—this time less hopeful—we took another shot at an ice cream outing. We weren't three hundred yards from the house when the kids started fighting again. I said, "That's 1, third time blows the trip." They hit a 2 and then a 3, and the car got turned around and headed for home.

I'm sure that before our next attempt at an evening treat the kids had had a conversation with each other. Their conversation probably went something like this: "Isn't it a shame that most children in the world, except us, have normal fathers? Unfortunately, our Dad turned out to be a shrink. But he's got the car and he's got the money, so if we want some ice cream, we'd better put up with his stupid games!"

So, about a week later, our intrepid group once again set out on its quest. To my amazement, the kids started fighting. As calmly as I could I said, "That's 1, third time blows the trip." To my further amazement the kids instantly became quiet and they were good as gold the whole rest of the way. We all enjoyed our dessert.

One moral of this story: Sometimes it takes a few trials for you to make believers out of the kids. By the way, I've often been asked what to do if while on the way one child acts up and the other one doesn't. The answer: The one gets the ice cream and the other one doesn't. But don't expect to enjoy the ride home.

Keep Moving

Another tactic that some parents have used successfully in public takes us back to our grocery store example, where the youngster was having a major fit in the candy section of aisle 5. What some parents have done is simply leave the child on the floor and move on to aisle 6. When they meet someone in aisle 6, they say, "Boy, do you hear all that racket over there?"

Seriously, what often happens is that the child starts worrying where Mom or Dad went, forgets the candy and runs to find his parent. Naturally, you wouldn't want to get too far away, depending on the age of the child. Then again, some kids run to find their parent and then remember the candy and continue the tantrum. What should you do then?

The answer to this question depends on two things: How badly do you need to shop and how much guts do you have? A number of years ago, I was shopping by myself in our local grocery store. I saw a lady come in with a four-year-old boy. She picked the boy up, put him in a cart and pushed the cart past the bubble-gum machine. The boy asked for gum, the mother said no and the boy went ballistic. The mother kept moving and said nothing.

I shopped for twenty minutes, this Mom shopped for twenty minutes, and this little boy howled for twenty minutes. Wherever you were in the store, which was not large, you could hear this kid's blood-curdling screams. But this lady was great. She paid no attention to her son. She had come in for milk, green pepper and converted rice, and, by God, she was going out with milk, green pepper and converted rice. I remember passing this duo in the rice aisle. While the youngster wailed, his mother was calmly looking at the rice box: "Let's see, four ounces times six. Yes, that should be enough for tonight."

I was impressed. But Mom was soon to fall off her pedestal. I hurried along because I wanted to get out of the noise-filled place. I got to the check-out line. The racket behind me started getting louder. There they were. This lady and her unhappy son got in the next line, and she checked out sooner than I did because she had fewer items. With great relief I watched her leaving the store, with her son still yelling. As she passed the bubble-gum machine for the second time, she stopped and bought her son a piece of gum!

I was dumbfounded. I almost lost all my professional decorum right there. I wanted to jump over the counter, run up to this woman, and say, "Excuse me, ma'am, you don't know me, but I'm a clinical psychologist. Could I talk to you for a moment?" This mother had just rewarded a twenty-minute tantrum.

There may be times out in public when, in spite of everything you've done, your child won't stop a tantrum. Your choices then are these: Gut it out and finish your shopping (you will feel foolish), take the child out to the car until he does stop screaming, or go home.

Don't Take Them Unless You Have To

Have you ever been to church on Sunday, and in the row ahead of you there is a couple with a two-year-old? The two-year-old, of course, isn't paying any attention to the service. Neither are his parents, since they are preoccupied with trying to keep their son in line so he won't bother other people. Finally, around this family trio are ten other individuals who aren't paying any attention to the service either, because they're busy evaluating how well the couple is disciplining their two-year-old.

So, in effect, we have thirteen people who might as well have not gone to church at all. Of course, we're not trying to talk you out of going to church, but think before you go anywhere. Don't ask for unnecessary trouble in public by putting your kids in situations they simply can't handle. In our church example, while the parents are trying their hardest not to allow their son to bother the other people around them, these other people are being distracted anyway.

Riding in the Car

Travelling in the car is a kind of half-public, half-private experience that can present parents with some extremely difficult and even dangerous situations. Travelling parents often feel like an unwilling captive audience to their children's misbehavior. And making matters worse, moms and dads also know their discipline options are limited.

Have you ever been riding along an interstate with your left hand on the steering wheel while your right hand is waving madly through the back seat trying to grab the kid who's just been teasing his sister for the fifty-seventh time since you left the last town? Vacations are supposed to be fun, but this kind of routine is not fun. I've had many parents tell me that they pretty much stopped taking vacations because of nasty and repeated scenes like these.

> **Quik Tip**
> Travelling in the car with the kids can be aggravating and that can also make it dangerous. Parents often feel like an unwilling but captive audience to their kids' misbehavior. Never fear! You have a number of tactics available to you.

Counting is very useful when chauffeuring the kids around town. The question, of course, is what to do at 3. Time-out alternatives are one choice. One couple, for example, didn't allow anyone to talk—including Mom and Dad—for fifteen minutes after the kids hit 3 for behavior like teasing, fighting or badgering. Other families have used fines (money taken off the allowance), at the rate of so many cents for each minute that would have been included in the child's normal time-out.

Being in the car, however, doesn't prevent you from doing a good-old-fashioned time-out. Where is the time-out room? You're riding in it! Your car is actually a stylish, gas-guzzling time-out room. Over the years a very effective tactic for many of my parents was 1-2-3, then pull the car off to the side of the road for the rest period. This strategy is dramatic and has quite an impact on the children.

For some reason, counting the kids in the car and having them serve the time-outs when they get home doesn't work as well, unless you're very close to home. The problem may be that the rest period comes too long after the offense. In addition, the demand for a time-out when you walk in the door may simply start another fight, because often by the time you get home everybody has forgotten the original problem.

On longer car rides and on vacations, counting can also be used effectively, just as it is with short trips. But other tactics are often helpful.

Other tactics that parents have used successfully in the car include the usual—and very helpful—activities like the alphabet game and car bingo. Putting one child in the front and one in the back can help, as can using a DVD player (and renting twenty movies!) or leaving at 4 in the morning so the kids sleep away the largest part of a four- or five-hour ride. Telling the kids they get fifty cents for every goat they see is also a brilliant maneuver.

The main point is this: Don't ever leave on a car ride with the kids— or especially on a long "vacation"—without putting on your thinking cap first. Have the 1-2-3 and a few other tactics in your hip pocket, because you're going to need them.

CHAPTER SUMMARY

Travelling with the kids?

Have a nice trip—
and put your thinking
cap on beforehand!

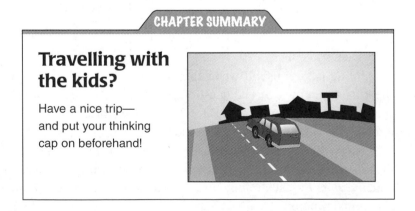

8

Sibling Rivalry, Tantrums and Pouting

Sibling rivalry: pastime for kids, torture for parents

Three common but aggravating childhood problems require a few minor modifications in our counting procedure. The first issue is sibling rivalry, which many parents put at the top of their List of Horribly Aggravating and Repetitive Behavior Problems. The other two are temper tantrums and pouting.

Sibling Rivalry

When you have more than one child acting up, your life has just become more complicated. Now there are multiple actors in the drama. How are you going to handle the situation? Sibling rivalry will never go away completely, but here are a few simple rules to follow:

Guideline 1: Count both kids. When the children are fighting, you should count both kids most of the time, unless one is the obvious, unprovoked aggressor. Usually they both helped produce the conflict. Be careful—kids are tricky! Some provoke in subtle ways and others in more overt ways, so it is often hard to tell who started a fight—even if you are right there.

For example, have you ever been driving in the car with the kids in the back and you hear, "Mom, he's looking at me again!'"? Who started that one? There's really no way to tell. So you count both children.

Guideline 2: Never ask the world's two stupidest questions. Every parent knows what these questions are: "What happened?" and "Who started it?" What do you expect to hear, a version of George Washington's "I cannot tell a lie"? "Yes, I started this fight and the last thirteen consecutive squabbles have also been my personal responsibility." That kind of confession won't happen. Instead, all you get is the kids blaming one another and yelling.

> **CAUTION**
>
> Never ask the world's two stupidest questions, "Who started it?" and "What happened?" unless you think someone is physically injured. Do you expect your kids to come up with George Washington's version of "I cannot tell a lie"?

There are, of course, times when you might need to ask what happened. If, for instance, you think someone might be physically injured, you would want to examine the child and find out what caused the injury. The same thing might be true with other serious or unusual cases. But for your run-of-the-mill sibling rivalry, trying to find out what happened is too often a lost cause.

Guideline 3: Don't expect an older child to act more mature during a fight than a younger child. Even if your two kids are eleven years old and four years old, don't say to the eleven-year-old, "She's only a baby; can't you put up with a little teasing?" That comment is the equivalent of loading the gun of the four-year-old, who will be sure to both appreciate your generosity and to take maximum advantage of it.

Along these same lines, imagine for a second that your eleven-year-old son comes up to you one day and says, "I want to ask you a question."

"Go ahead," you say.

"How come I always get a ten-minute time-out, and Miss Shrimp over there (your four-year-old) only has to go for five minutes?"

"Because the rule in our house," you say, "is one minute of time-out for each year of your life."

"WELL THAT'S THE DUMBEST THING I EVER HEARD OF!"

"That's 1."

This child doesn't really want information, he wants a fight. But don't get sidetracked into a useless argument. With *1-2-3 Magic* we have a rule that goes: Count attacks and discuss discussions.

What if the kids have a fight and they share the same room? It would not be a good idea to send two fighting children to the same time-out place to continue their fight. Send one to his room and the other to an alternate time-out room or place. Then for the next rest period reverse the locations. Or use time-out alternatives when both children fight. If your kids have separate bedrooms and they fight on the way to their rest periods, extend the time-outs by five or ten minutes.

Temper Tantrums

Tantrums can be counted or ignored. You might choose to ignore your two-year-old's thrashing around on the living room floor after you refused to give him your entire milkshake. You can even leave the room if you think the youngster will be safe. But you might want to count your ten-year-old's verbal abuse after you wouldn't let him have a friend over.

In either case, there is a basic rule about dealing with fits of temper: *Never talk or argue with a tantruming child.* That's the same as pouring gasoline on a fire. Counting is OK because it's really just a signal rather than a conversation.

So let's say you chose to time-out your six-year-old son for tantruming. He's now in his room and he's still having a fit. What if the time-out period is up but the child's not done with the tantrum? You don't want to let him out in his condition and, in a sense, he's just earned another time-out. The answer to this dilemma, fortunately, is simple: If the child is four or older, the time-out doesn't start until the tantrum is over. So if it takes the youngster fifteen minutes to calm down, the rest period starts after fifteen minutes. And if it takes the kid two hours to calm down (could be a room-wrecker!), the time-out starts after two hours.

Don't be sticking your head in his room every five or ten minutes saying things like, "Come on now, don't you think that's enough? We miss you. Dinner's in five minutes and you have homework to do." Just leave him alone until he's tired of being angry.

The only children we don't use this temper-tantrum modification for are the two- and three-year-olds. They don't seem to get the idea, so just let them out after a couple of minutes, even if they're still tantruming, and cross your fingers. Once they're out, ignoring the child is usually more effective than trying to talk him out of his irritation. If he still doesn't quiet down, leave him in a little longer the next time.

One caution. Some kids will tantrum due to sensory issues. Their socks or shoes or sweater literally rubs them the wrong way. These sensory irritabilities are not misbehavior, nor does the child choose to be this way. Take the child's opinions seriously, and try to avoid the offending smells, tastes or feels.

Pouting

Pouting is a passive behavior that is designed to make you feel guilty. If you do feel guilty when your child pouts, that's really more your problem. Why should you feel bad for trying to be a good parent? Remember: The demanding/firm part of parenting is essential.

So if you discipline a child and she gives you the ultimate in martyr looks, just turn around, say nothing and walk away. The only time you would do something different is if you get what we call an "aggressive pouter." An aggressive pouter is a child who follows you all over the house to make sure you don't miss a minute of the sour face. If she does that, "That's 1." She's trying to rub your nose in her grumpiness, and you're not going to allow her to do that.

CHAPTER SUMMARY

Points to Remember

1. SIBLING RIVALRY: Count both kids most of the time.

2. TEMPER TANTRUMS: The time-out doesn't start until after the tantrum is over.

3. POUTING: Pouting can be ignored unless the child becomes an "aggressive pouter."

9
Getting Started with Counting

Under New Management

A question often asked at seminars is this: Do you explain to the kids what you're going to be doing? The answer is yes. Starting the 1-2-3 is pretty easy. The Kickoff Conversation only takes about five minutes and a little rehearsing only takes a few minutes more. But don't put a lot of stock in the impact of this initial conversation. Wishful thinking on your part will not do the job. Lots of children don't really get the idea until they've been counted for a while, been to their rooms a few times, or until after they've seen their sibs counted.

If both parents are living at home, or even if Mom and Dad live in separate places, it's preferable if both grownups sit down together with the youngsters and do the initial explaining. If you have an ex, however, and *you don't get along*, do the Kickoff separately or you'll ruin it.

The Kickoff Conversation

Here's what you say: "Listen, you guys know there are times when you do things we don't care for, like arguing, whining and teasing. From now on we're going to do something different. When we see you doing something you're not supposed to, we'll say, 'That's 1.' That's a warning, and it means you're supposed to stop. If you don't stop, we'll say, 'That's 2.' That will be your second warning. If you still don't stop, we'll say, 'That's 3, take 5 (or however many minutes equals your age).' That means you have to go to your room for a time-out. It's like a kind of rest period. When you come out, we don't talk about what happened unless it's really necessary. We just forget it and start over.

"By the way, kids, there's part of this new system that you'll like and part you won't like. Here's what you won't like: If the thing you do is bad enough to start with, like swearing or hitting, we'll say, 'That's 3, take 10 or 15.' That means there aren't any other warnings, you just go straight to your room, and the time will be longer.

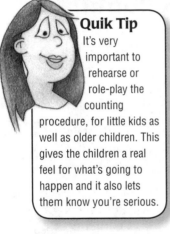

Quik Tip

It's very important to rehearse or role-play the counting procedure, for little kids as well as older children. This gives the children a real feel for what's going to happen and it also lets them know you're serious.

"The part you will like is that most of the time we won't talk about what happened after a time-out. Well, that's the new deal. It's pretty simple. Do you have any questions?"

Expect the kids to sit there and look at you like you've just gone off your rocker. Some kids will poke each other and exchange knowing glances, as if to say, "Well, it looks like Mom went to the library again and got another one of those books on how to raise us guys. Last time she stuck to it for about four days, and Dad never did anything different at all. I think if we stick together and hang tough, we should be running the house again inside of a week, right?"

Wrong. Don't expect the children to be grateful, to look enlightened or to thank you for your efforts to raise them responsibly. Just get going, stick to your guns and—when in doubt—count!

Dress Rehearsal

Now you can have some fun. Since some two-, three- and four-year-olds won't understand everything you've just said, it's a good idea to rehearse or role play counting for them. It's also very important, however, to rehearse with the older children too. Just saying the Kickoff is somewhat like a Little Adult explanation. Rehearsing the procedure gives the kids a *feel* for what's going to happen and also tells the children *you're serious*.

Here's what you say next: "Kids, let's practice counting. Who wants to start? OK, Kieran, pretend you're whining at me for candy. Can you do a good whine? (Kid whines). Wow, that was a good whine! Now I'll say, 'That's 1.' Now whine again ..." And so on.

Now take them through the rest of the procedure, so they get a feel for being counted, hitting three, getting to the time-out room or chair, serving the time (abbreviate the time-out), and then being let out. Make sure you praise them in an age-appropriate way for their cooperation.

Other possible role plays: The little ones can count a stuffed animal. Mom and Dad can count each other (one pretends to be a misbehaving kid). The kids can count you and you go to time-out. While on your way to time-out, don't go like a goodie two shoes. Grumble a little! The message: It's OK to not like being counted and going to time-out.

At this point, you may feel that you're ready to start using the 1-2-3. Not so fast! If you began counting right now, you wouldn't be prepared for the fact that many children—about half—are going to give you a hard time in the beginning. That may be the bad news, but the good news is that we're on to the youngsters now! We have discovered and identified the Six Kinds of Testing and Manipulation. Once you understand these tactics and what's behind them, you'll be ready for anything.

CHAPTER SUMMARY

You're almost ready to begin your first giant parenting step:

Controlling Obnoxious Behavior!

Part III

Managing Kids'
Testing and Manipulation

Chapter 10

**The Six Types of
Testing and Manipulation**

Chapter 11

Counting in Action

Chapter 12

More Serious Offenses in Tweens

10

The Six Types of
Testing and Manipulation

You call off your dogs, and I'll call off mine.

When you are in the warm/friendly parenting mode, you will not usually be frustrating your children. When you are operating from the demanding/firm side, however, you will be! You have to regularly frustrate your youngsters in three main ways: 1) asking them to start doing things they don't want to do (homework, going to bed), 2) asking them to stop doing things they do want to do (teasing, whining), and 3) not giving them something they want (cookie, toy).

When you are frustrating your little ones, the children have two choices. First, they can cooperate and tolerate the frustration. Most kids gradually learn that frustration is not the end of the world, and as they mature they begin to get a sense that putting up with present aggravations may actually be the route to future rewards. That—the ability to delay gratification now for something better later—is one foundation of emotional intelligence.

On the other hand, however, frustrated youngsters can engage in what we call *testing and manipulation*. Testing and manipulation are the efforts of the less-powerful child to get what he wants or to avoid discipline by getting his parent emotionally confused and, consequently, sidetracked.

Three things need to be remembered about testing:

1. *Testing occurs when a child is frustrated.* You are not giving him the potato chips he wants; you are counting him; you are making him do homework or go to bed. He doesn't like this and hopes for a way to get what he wants in spite of you.

2. *Testing, therefore, is purposeful behavior.* The primary purpose of a child's testing, obviously, is to get his way rather than have you impose your will on him. If the child still doesn't get his way, testing and manipulation can have a secondary purpose: *revenge.* You don't give me what I want, you're going to pay.

3. *When engaging in testing and manipulation, a child has a "choice" of six basic tactics.* All six can serve the primary purpose: getting one's way; five of the six tactics can serve the secondary purpose: revenge. Often a child's testing behavior will represent a combination of one or more of the basic tactics.

All parents will recognize the manipulative tactics we are about to describe. These adults have encountered these ploys of children many times. Grownups are also usually aware—if they think about it—of which maneuvers are used by which children. Moms and dads may also recognize some of their own favorite strategies, since adults use the same basic manipulative methods.

Key Concept

The first goal of testing is for the child to get what he wants. Since he's less powerful than you are, he must use some emotional manipulation. If the child still fails to get what he wants, the second goal of testing is often retaliation or revenge. The kid is going to make you pay!

By the way, the use of testing and manipulation does not mean that a child is sick, emotionally troubled or in need of psychological care. Attempts to get your way, as well as attempts to "punish" the bigger people who don't give you your way, are perfectly normal. The use of testing also does not require an exceptionally high IQ. In fact, adults are often amazed at how naturally and how skillfully little kids are able to produce, as well as modify, complex testing strategies. Because our sons and daughters are so naturally skilled, it is very important that adult caretakers understand children's testing and how to manage it.

The Six Basic Testing Tactics

Here are the six fundamental strategies that children use to attempt to influence the adults who are frustrating them:

1. Badgering: "Why? Why? Why? Why?"

Badgering is the "Please, please, please, please!" or "Why, why, why?" routine. "Just this once! Just this once! Just this once! Just this once!" "Mom! Mom! Mom! Mom! Mom!" There are some children who could have been machine guns during the last war. The child keeps after you and after you and after you, trying to wear you down with repetition. "Just give me what I want and I'll shut up!" is the underlying message.

Badgering can be particularly taxing when it is done loudly and when it is done in public. Some parents attempt to respond to everything the frustrated child says every time she says it. Mom or Dad may try to explain, to reassure or to distract. As badgering continues, though, parents can become more and more desperate, going on the equivalent of a verbal wild goose chase—searching for the right words or reasons to make the youngster keep quiet. Many kids, however, are extremely single-minded once their badgering starts. They won't stop until they either get what they want or until their parent uses a more effective approach to stop the testing. We'll soon clarify exactly what that approach will be.

Badgering is what we refer to as a great "blender" tactic, since it mixes easily with other manipulative strategies. The basic element in badgering, of course, is repetition. So when any of the other verbal testing tactics are repeated again and again, the resulting manipulative strategy is a combination of that other tactic plus the repetitive power of badgering.

2. Temper (Intimidation): "I HATE YOU!"

Displays of temper, or what we sometimes refer to as intimidation, involve obvious, aggressive behavior. Younger children, who aren't so adept at words, may throw themselves on the floor, bang their heads, holler at the top of their lungs and kick around ferociously. Older kids, whose language skills are developed, may come up with arguments that accuse you of being unjust, illogical or simply a bad parent in general. When frustrated, older kids may also swear or complain angrily.

Some children's fits of temper go on for very long periods. Many ADHD and bipolar children, for example, have been known to rant and rave for more than an hour at a time. In the process they may damage property or trash their rooms. Tantrums will be prolonged 1) if the child has an audience, 2) if the adults involved continue talking, arguing or pleading with the youngster or 3) if the adults don't know what to do.

Temper fits in two-year-olds can be aggravating, but they can also be funny. My wife took a picture of our son when he was an energetic toddler having a temper tantrum right in the middle of the ashes in the fireplace at my parents' home (the fire was not going, of course). We all can still laugh at that scene.

As kids get older and more powerful, however, tantrums get more worrisome and just plain scarier. That's why we like to see them well controlled or eliminated by the time a child is five or six.

3. Threat: "I'm going to run away from home!"

Frustrated kids often threaten their parents with dire predictions if the adults don't come across with the desired goods. Here are a few examples:

"I'm going to run away from home!"
"I'll never speak to you again!"
"I'm going to kill myself!"
"I'm not eating dinner and I won't
   do my homework!!"
"I'm going to kill the parakeet!"

The message is clear: Something bad is going to happen unless you give me what I want immediately. Give me the Twinkie right before dinner, stop counting me, don't make me go to bed, OR ELSE! Some of the threats that younger children come up with are funny. One little girl, whose mother was trying to get her to go to bed, angrily shouted, "All right, I'll go. But I'm going to lie there all night with my eyes open!"

Another six-year-old boy was counted and timed out by his father for squirting the dog with a hose. The boy threatened to run away, actually packed a small bag and walked out the front door. After five minutes, however, he walked back in the door and yelled at his Dad, "I couldn't run away because you guys won't let me cross the street!"

Other threats are not funny. Some frustrated children threaten to kill themselves, and this is something no parent takes lightly. Parents wonder if this is just manipulative or if their child really wants to die. Two questions can help parents sort out this dilemma. First of all, is this child generally happy? Does she enjoy life most of the time, have friends, do OK in school and fit into the family? If the answers to these questions are positive, it is less likely that the child wants to end her life. Second, did the suicidal threat come out of the blue or was the comment a response to some obvious, recent frustration? If "I'm going to kill myself" comes out of nowhere, the threat is always more worrisome and needs to be looked into.

4. Martyrdom: "I never get anything!"

Martyr-like testing tactics are a perennial favorite of children. When using martyrdom, the child may indicate that his life has become totally unfair and an incredible burden. "No one around here loves me anymore," "I never get anything" or "You like her more than me" are examples.

Or the youngster may actually do something that has a self-punitive, self-denying flavor, such as not eating dinner, sitting in the closet for an hour or staring out the window without talking. Crying, pouting and simply looking sad or teary can also be useful manipulative devices.

The goal of martyrdom, obviously, is to make the parent feel guilty, and martyrdom can be surprisingly effective. This testing tactic is very difficult for adults to handle. Many moms and dads seem to have a "guilt button" the size of the state of Wyoming! All the kids have to do is push that button and the youngsters wind up running the house.

Children learn early on that parents are highly invested in the welfare of their offspring. Kids know their caretakers want them safe, happy and healthy. Unfortunately, kids also seem to naturally appreciate a logical consequence of this adult commitment: Acting hurt or deprived can be a powerful way of influencing adult behavior.

Two-year-olds, for example, will sometimes hold their breath till they turn blue when they are mad about not getting what they want. Many parents wonder how a child can even come up with an idea like that. One creative child, whose mother had just sent her to her bedroom, was heard yelling out her window, "I can't breathe! I can't breathe!" This tactic may have been creative, but it was not effective.

What's Going On Here?

Before we finish our list of the Six Kinds of Testing and Manipulation, let's stop and figure out what this commotion is all about. Just exactly what are the kids trying to accomplish with these maneuvers, and how do they think the process will work?

> **Quik Tip**
> A child who is testing you is offering you a deal: Give me what I want and my badgering, temper, threat or martyrdom will stop—immediately! Does that sound like a deal you can't refuse? Think again!

Most kids, of course, would never be able to describe the underlying mechanics of testing. But we can tell you *exactly* what's going on. Here's how it works: The first four tactics—badgering, intimidation, threat and martyrdom—share a common dynamic. The child, without quite knowing what he's doing, is in effect saying to the parent: "Look, you're making me uncomfortable by not giving me what I want. You're making me get out of bed, you're counting me for teasing my sister or you're not buying me a treat. But now I'm also making you uncomfortable with my badgering, tantrums, ominous statements or feeling sorry for myself. *Now that we're both uncomfortable, I'll make you a deal: You call off your dogs and I'll call off mine.*"

If you do give in and give the child what he wants, you are guaranteed that any testing will stop immediately. In a split second, no more hassles. Some people say, "Thank heaven—there's a way of getting rid of testing and manipulation!" There certainly is, but what's the catch? The catch, of course, is who's running your house? It certainly isn't you; it's the kids. All they have to do during a conflict is get out their big manipulative guns and you are chopped liver.

Now let's finish our list of testing tactics. The last two, when compared to each other, are like day and night.

5. Butter Up: "You're the nicest Dad in the world!"

The fifth tactic, butter up, takes an approach that's different from the first four. Instead of making you feel uncomfortable, with butter up the child tries to make you feel good. You may then run the risk of losing this good feeling if you subsequently frustrate the child.

"Gee, Mom, you've got the prettiest eyes of anybody on the block" is a fairly blatant example. Or, "I think I'll go clean my room. It's been looking kind of messy for the last three weeks. And after that maybe I'll take a look at the garage."

With butter up the basic message from child to parent is: "You'll feel really bad if you mistreat or discipline or deny me after how nice I've been to you." Butter up is intended to be an advance set-up for parental guilt. The child is implying, "You'll feel so positively toward me that you won't have the heart to make me feel bad."

Promises can be used by children as butter-up manipulation. "Please, Mom. Please. I'll eat my dinner and I promise I won't even ask for any dessert," said one little girl who wanted a snack at 5 in the afternoon. Some promises kids make are impossibilities. One little boy, while in the process of pressing his father for a new computer, said, "I'll never ask you for anything ever again."

Apologies can be sincere, and they can also be examples of butter-up testing. "I'm sorry, I'm sorry. I said I'm sorry," one little boy pleaded in an attempt to avoid a grounding for socking his little brother.

Butter-up manipulation is obviously the least obnoxious of all the testing tactics. Some people, in fact, don't think it should be labeled as testing at all. It is true that butter up is sometimes hard to distinguish from genuine affection. If a child says "I love you" and then proceeds not to ask for anything, it's probably genuine affection. And a child who asks if he can have a friend over if he cleans up his room may be proposing a straightforward and legitimate deal. But if you've ever heard a parent say, "The only time my son's ever nice is when he wants something," that person is probably referring to butter up.

6. Physical Tactics: Pow! Whack! Bam!

From a parent's perspective, this last form of testing is perhaps the worst strategy of all. Here the frustrated child may physically attack an adult, break something or run away. Physical methods of trying to get one's way, of course, are more common in smaller children who don't have well developed language skills. When the use of this type of testing continues beyond age four or five, however, we begin to worry. Some kids have a long history of this kind of behavior, and the bigger the child gets, the scarier their use of physical strategies gets.

Some parents who use time-outs, for example, tell us that their children sometimes physically attack them when the parent is trying to escort the child to the time-out area. (Any child who is mad enough to assault his parent is certainly not going to go voluntarily to his room.) Some youngsters become quite ferocious, kicking, biting, scratching, pinching and hitting while yelling at the top of their lungs.

Other frustrated, physically oriented kids will smash or break things—sometimes even their own possessions. One ten-year-old boy, for instance, was sent to his room for fighting with his brother. The door to his bedroom happened to be shut when he got to it, so he gave it one of his best karate kicks, cracking the door down the middle. Another lad smashed a coffee mug on the tile floor in the front hall of the house. Unfortunately, one of the larger pieces of the mug went flying into the glass storm door, which promptly disintegrated.

Another physical testing tactic, running away, is not used a lot by younger children. Threats to run away appear more often in this age group. One seven-year-old boy, though, used a different version of this idea on his mother, who had just denied his request to go outside. The boy sneaked down to the basement and hid for two hours, not responding to anyone who called his name. The tactic was effective, at least in punishing his mother, who was beside herself with worry.

Badgering, temper, threat, martyrdom, butter up and physical tactics. These are the methods children use to get their way from adults. And all these tactics, except butter up, can also be used by kids to punish the uncooperative adults who obstinately persist in refusing to give the youngsters what they want.

We have taken several surveys of parents and teachers, asking which tactics they thought children used the most. Interestingly, both groups of grownups always mention the same three: badgering, temper and—the overwhelming favorite—martyrdom.

You will also be interested to know that the most annoying manipulative maneuver used by children is a tactic that combines two of the above three favorites. This tactic, which drives many parents absolutely nuts, is a combination of martyrdom (#4) and badgering (#1). The word describing it starts with the letter W. You guessed it: Whining! Whining is the old 4-1 routine.

Who's Pushing Your Buttons?

Now we're going to ask you a very important question. Think of each of your kids, one at a time, and ask yourself, "Does this child have a favorite testing tactic? One that he or she uses very frequently or all the time?" If your answer is yes, that's bad. Why? Because the testing ploy *works* for the youngster. People don't generally repeat behavior that doesn't work for them.

What does "works" mean? All you have to do is recall the two purposes of testing and manipulation. First of all, a testing strategy works when the child successfully gets his way by using that tactic. How do you know if a child is getting his way by testing? It's obvious—you just give it to him. You give him the snack right before dinner, turn the TV back on while he's doing homework, stop counting him when he's teasing the dog or don't make him go to bed.

"Works" can also refer to the second purpose of testing and manipulation: revenge.

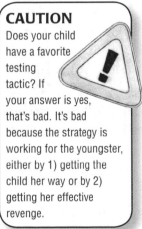

CAUTION
Does your child have a favorite testing tactic? If your answer is yes, that's bad. It's bad because the strategy is working for the youngster, either by 1) getting the child her way or by 2) getting her effective revenge.

Children will repeat tactics that provide an effective way of retaliating against the adults who are causing the frustration. How does a child know if she is effectively getting revenge? The answer takes us right back to the No-Talking, No-Emotion Rules. If this child can get you very upset and get you talking too much, she knows she's got you.

Youngsters know they are getting effective revenge when their parents start talking like this: "How many times do I have to tell you?!" "Why can't you just take no for an answer?!" "ARE YOU TRYING TO DRIVE ME NUTS?!" The angry part of your frustrated child will find comments like these satisfying, and the next time your child is angry with you, he will know exactly how to press the revenge button.

You want some homework done, for example, and your son has a tantrum (Tactic #2) because he wants to watch TV. Your response, however, is a *counter* temper tantrum. You get more upset than your son did! Final score: Child 5, Parent 2. He got you: The small, inferior part of the youngster got the angry big splash from the larger, "more powerful" adult.

Other kids retaliate by making their parents feel guilty. Imagine that your daughter—when asked to go to bed—resorts to martyrdom (Tactic #4): "Well, it's obvious that nobody around here loves me anymore. I might as well hitchhike to the next state and find a family more compatible with my basic needs." Here she adds a touch of threat, Tactic #3. You feel frightened and guilty. You are certain that unloved children grow up to be mentally ill, homeless or serial killers. You sit the youngster down on your lap, and for a half hour tell her how much you love her, how much Dad and the dog love her, and so on.

You have just been had by Tactic #4, Martyrdom. You are squirming and uncomfortable, and your child is making you pay for your parenting sins. Always remember this: Unless you are a grossly neglectful or abusive parent, your kids know that you love them. By all means tell them that you love them, but never tell them that you love them when they're pulling a #4 on you.

How to Manage Testing and Manipulation

Now let's say you're getting into the spirit of *1-2-3 Magic* and you're toughening up some. Your ten-year-old son wants to go to a friend's house at 9 on a school night. You deny his request and tell him it's too late. The following scene occurs:

"Why not? Come on, just this once!" (Badgering)
"Can't do it."

"I never get anything." (Martyrdom, Badgering)
"I don't think you're too underprivileged."
"I'll clean the garage tomorrow." (Butter Up, Badgering)
"The garage is OK the way it is. I just cleaned it."
"This stinks—I HATE YOUR GUTS!" (Intimidation, Badgering)
"Sorry."
The child throws a book on the floor. (Physical Tactic)
"Watch your step, pal."
"Please, PLEASE! Oh, come on, it's not so late." (Badgering)
"No way. Not tonight."
"If you don't let me, I'm running away!" (Threat, Badgering)

This may be aggravating, but in a way it's good! Why? Because something constructive is happening. The child is fishing around, switching tactics and probing for your weak spot. *But he can't find a weak spot.* You are sticking to your guns. Not only that, you are remaining fairly calm in spite of the aggravation.

There is one thing wrong with this example, however, and that has to do with how you handle testing and manipulation. You would not let the child switch tactics that many times (and you would also not talk so much). What should you do, then? Well, if you look at our list of six testing tactics, five of them (except butter up) are Stop behavior. Stop behavior should be counted. So if a child were pushing you this much, he would be counted.

This is how the scene above should be handled if you were using the 1-2-3. Remember that the boy has already been given an explanation:

"Why not? Come on, just this once!" (Badgering)
"That's 1."
"I never get anything." (Martyrdom, Badgering)
"That's 2."
"I'll clean the garage tomorrow." (Butter Up, Badgering)
"That's 3, take 10."

The third count is more for the badgering than the butter up, but it's obvious this kid's not going to give up until the parent gently but firmly puts his foot down. That goal is achieved by counting.

Remember: With the exceptions of butter up and passive pouting, testing and manipulation should be counted, especially in the beginning when you're just starting *1-2-3 Magic*. Once the kids are used to the discipline system, the less aggressive, less obnoxious forms of testing can—at your discretion—occasionally be ignored. The effectiveness of not responding at all (verbally or nonverbally) to a child's testing can be evaluated by how quickly the child gives up the battle. Many kids will quickly learn that no response at all from you (ignoring) means that this time they are not going to either get their way or get effective revenge.

What to Expect in the Beginning

As we mentioned before, once you start counting, the kids will fall primarily into two categories: immediate cooperators and immediate testers. Immediate cooperators you simply enjoy. You will feel more affectionate toward your youngsters because they are listening to you. You will want to have more fun with your kids, talk with them, praise them and listen to them. You will enjoy working on building a good relationship. This good relationship, in turn, will make counting 1) less necessary and 2) a lot easier when it is necessary.

Immediate testers, however, get worse at first. When you let them know you're going to be the boss and you take away the power of their favorite testing strategies, these children deteriorate in two ways. Some will *up the ante* with a particular testing tactic. The volume and length of a child's tantrums, for example, may double. Badgering may become more intense or aggressive, and martyrdom may become more whiney and pathetic.

The other unpleasant change you may see initially in noncooperators is *tactic switching*. The kids may try new manipulative strategies you've not seen before, or they may return to others they haven't used for years. The most common switches involve going from badgering and martyrdom (and whining!) to temper. Some kids, quite understandably, blow up when their attempts to wear you down with repetition or make you feel guilty fail. Although tactic switching is aggravating, remember that switching is almost always a sign that you are doing well at sticking to your guns. Keep it up!

What do you do when faced with tactic escalation and tactic switching? Several things are important: 1) Don't get discouraged; this is a normal stage children go through while adjusting to *1-2-3 Magic*, 2) Count when necessary, 3) Keep your mouth shut except for necessary explanations and the counting itself. Eventually tactic escalation and tactic switching will diminish and your youngsters will accept your discipline without having a major cow every time you have to frustrate them. You then have won the battle. You are the parent, they are the children, and your home is a more peaceful place.

One final word: Some kids, after cooperating initially, become "delayed testers" later on. Delayed testing can occur after the novelty of the new system wears off, when the youngsters begin to realize that they aren't getting their way anymore, or if your routine gets disrupted by travel, visitors, illness, new babies or just plain time.

If you're unprepared for it, delayed testing can be a bit disillusioning. You think to yourself, "The kids were so good before!" You may feel like the whole system is falling apart, or that it was too good to be true. Fortunately, the remedy is not far away. Read *1-2-3 Magic* again, watch the DVD, discuss the suggestions with your spouse if possible, then get back to basics: No Talking, No Emotion, be gentle but aggressive and when in doubt, count. Things should shape up quickly.

CHAPTER SUMMARY

Kid's All-Time Favorite Tactic?

The 4-1 Pattern:
Whining!

11
Counting in Action

1-2-3 Magic reality show

Now let's study some examples of the 1-2-3 in action to give you a feel for how and when counting can be used. Our stories and commentaries will illustrate some of the basic do's and don'ts involved with the procedure. In some of our examples, when our parents don't do so well with their discipline the first time around, we'll give them a chance to correct their mistakes. Wouldn't it be nice if you had that opportunity in real life? Guess what? You do.

Sibling Rivalry

Like most siblings, nine-year-old John and seven-year-old Brittany are best of friends and best of enemies. They are doing Legos on the living room floor. Dad is watching the football game on TV and so far is amazed the kids are getting along so well, but the fun is about to end.

"Brittany, I need another wheel for my tank," says John sweetly.

"No, John, I've got it on my wagon," says Brittany nervously.

(Dad squirms in his chair. It's fourth-and-goal for the good guys.)

"Lemme just use one wheel now. I'll give it back to you later," suggests brother.

"No, my wagon needs four wheels," replies sister.

"Your wagon looks stupid!"

"Dad, John's gonna take one of my wheels and I had them first!"
  (Dad's team had to try for a field goal and it was blocked. Dad
  is not pleased.)

"Both of you, knock it off!"

"She doesn't need to hog all the wheels. There aren't enough
  for me to make what I want, and they're my Legos."

"But I made this first!"

"OK, kids, that's 1 for both of you."

"She's an idiot." (John smashes his creation and leaves.)

Comment: Pretty good discipline job by Dad. Perhaps he should have counted a little bit sooner instead of growling "Knock it off!" Should Dad have counted John for smashing his tank or badmouthing his sister? Some parents would count these behaviors, but others wouldn't because the tank was John's (and it can be rebuilt). John may also be doing the right thing by leaving the situation.

Second chance: Let's give Dad another chance to improve his parenting technique:

"Brittany, I need another wheel for my tank," says John sweetly.

"No, John, I've got it on my wagon," says Brittany nervously.
  (Dad squirms in his chair. It's fourth-and-goal for the good guys.)

"Lemme just use one wheel now. I'll give it back to you later,"
  suggests brother.

"No, my wagon needs four wheels," replies sister.

"Your wagon looks stupid!"

"Kids, that's 1 for both of you."
  (Dad's team had to try for a field goal and it was blocked. Dad is
  not pleased.)

"She doesn't need to hog all the wheels. There aren't enough
  for me to make what I want, and they're my Legos."

"But I made this first!"

"OK, kids, that's 2."

Comment: Dad did much better this time, especially since he was extra aggravated after his team blew its scoring opportunity. Excellent self-control and an excellent job of not taking his extra frustration out on the kids.

Four-Year-Old Speeding

Rita is four years old and she loves to go shopping at the grocery store with her Mom. The reason she loves shopping trips is because the store has little kiddie carts she can push around just like her mother does. Rita's Mom, however, does not enjoy shopping with her daughter as much as vice versa. The reason Mom does not like these shopping trips is because, sooner or later, Rita always starts running around with the cart. Last week the little girl ran into the big shopping cart of an older gentleman. Although the man was nice about it and even laughed, Mom is afraid her daughter will hurt someone.

Talk about the devil and the deep blue sea! If Mom doesn't let Rita have a cart, the girl will throw a raging fit—guaranteed—in front of everyone in the store. Mom feels her daughter is running the show.

Mom is correct. Here's how the scene goes when Mom and Rita enter the store:

"Mom! Can I push a cart?"

"I don't think so, dear. Not today. Look at the Fuzzy Bear sign!"

"Why can't I?"

"I just told you, dear. Now please don't start giving me a hard time."

"I wanna push my own one!"

"Now stop that! That's enough! Come on, we've got a lot of things to get."

"I never get to do anything!" Rita starts crying loudly.

"OK, OK! Stop that!" Mom gets a kiddie cart for Rita. Rita grabs the cart, but Mom holds the cart for a second and looks at her daughter firmly.

"Rita, look at me. You have to promise me you won't run with the cart. You might hurt someone. Do you understand me?"

"Yes."

"And you promise you won't run with the cart?"

"Yes."

"Say I promise."

"I promise."

"OK. Now let's get our stuff. I'll put some things in your cart."

Rita does just fine for six minutes. Then she starts running with her kiddie cart, giggling as she zooms past the spaghetti sauce. Her mother pretends she doesn't notice, then she cuts the shopping trip short after getting only one-third of the things she needed. Maybe she can come back later and get the rest of what she wants by herself.

Comment: A classic example of a child intimidating a parent with the threat of public embarrassment. Mom is intimidated into a desperate attempt at little-adult reasoning ("You might hurt someone") and the elicitation of futile promises.

Let's give Mom another chance to get this one right. Actually, Rita's mother has two choices: 1) counting Rita for speeding and at count 3 taking away the cart, and 2) not letting Rita have a cart in the first place.

Option 1: Counting Rita for speeding

"Mom! Can I push a cart?"

"Yes, dear. But you have to walk with it. If I count you to 3 for running, I'll take the cart away."

Rita does fine for three minutes, then starts running with the kiddie cart.

"Rita, that's 1. At 3 you lose the cart."

Comment: This approach is much better. There will probably be hell to pay if Rita hits 3, so Mom should be ready to take the little girl out to the car for a while till she finishes her tantrum. If returning to the car is necessary, no parental "I told you so" comments are allowed.

Option 2: Not letting Rita have the kiddie cart

"Mom! Can I push a cart?"

"No. Last time you ran with it."

"Why can't I?"

"That's 1."

"I wanna push my own one!"

"That's 2."

Comment: Good work, Mom!

Dog Teasing

Four-year-old Michael has the dog backed into a corner and pushed up against the wall. The dog, normally patient, looks uncomfortable. Mom intervenes.

"Michael, please don't tease the dog, honey."
(Michael giggles and continues pushing the dog against the wall.)
"That's 1."
"No! I wanna pet him." (For the first time, the dog snarls.)
"That's 3, take 5. The dog is mad and could bite."
"I WANNA PET HIM!" (Michael falls on floor, releasing the dog, but yelling and crying. Mom drags the unwilling body to the bedroom for time-out.)

Comment: Couldn't have done it better. When the dog snarled, Mom went straight to 3 because of the danger. No talking while "escorting" the child to the rest period.

Bedtime Problem

It's nine o'clock in the evening. Alex is playing an electronic game on the couch in the living room. His mother enters the room:

"Alex, it's time to get ready for bed."
Entranced with his game, Alex does not respond at all.
"Alex, That's 1."

Comment: Should counting be used for bedtime? No. Getting ready for bed is a Start behavior—actually, a series of Start behaviors that take a while to complete. Counting is for obnoxious behavior, such as whining, arguing, teasing or tantrums, where cooperation takes only a few seconds. For bedtime, this Mom needs a bedtime routine (see Chapter 18).

Requests

Eight-year-old Tom asks his mother if he can use his Dad's electric jigsaw in the basement tool room.

"I don't think so. You better wait till Daddy's home."
"Oh come on, Mom. I know how to do it."

"No, I think it's too dangerous."

"There's nothing else to do." (Badgering, Martyrdom)

"I said no. That's 1."

"THAT'S 1! THAT'S 2! THAT'S 3! THAT'S 12! THAT'S
20! THAT'S STUPID!" (Intimidation)

"That's 2."

"Didn't know you could count that high." (Intimidation)

"That's 3, take 10 and add 5 for the mouth."

"Gee, I'll need a calculator for this one."

Mom moves toward Tom to escort him if necessary, but he goes to his bedroom.

Comment: Mom did very well—one explanation and then she counted. Mom also adds five for the smart mouth, and she has the presence of mind to stay cool in spite of the insult. When her son doesn't go to the rest period right away, she also does not get caught up in a stupid argument or little-adult conversation.

Interrupting

Mom and Dad are having a private conversation on the couch about the recent hospitalization of Mom's father. Seven-year-old Michelle jumps in between them.

"Hi, guys!"

"Hi, honey. Listen, Mom and Dad have to talk about something
very important for a few minutes, so you go play for a little bit."

"I wanna be here with you. I promise I won't listen."

"No, dear. Come on now, you go and play."

"I don't have anything to do." (Badgering)

"Listen, young lady. We're not going to tell you again!"

"THERE'S NOTHING ELSE FOR ME TO DO!" (Intimidation)

"Do you want a spanking!?"

(Michelle starts crying. Martyrdom)

"OK, that's 1."

(Michelle leaves, crying.)

Comment: Pretty sloppy job by Mom and Dad. In fairness to these parents, this is a touchy situation because Michelle's entrance is very friendly and these parents don't want to tell her what they're discussing just yet. They only get around to counting after ridiculous attempts at persuasion, threatening a spanking and risking World War III for nothing. They eventually recover and count, but some damage has still been done.

Second chance: Let's take it from the top:

"Hi, guys!"

"Hi, honey. Listen, Mom and Dad have to talk about something
  very important for a few minutes, so you go play for a little bit."

"I wanna be here with you. I promise I won't listen."

"That's 1."

"I don't have anything to do." (Badgering)

"That's 2."

Michelle leaves, a bit teary.

Comment: Mom and Dad probably feel a little bit guilty, but they handled the situation well. You can't give the kids everything.

1-2-3, Separate!

Joey, 8, and Maddie, 6, are in the family room. Joey is playing with his dinosaurs and Maddie is working on a puzzle. Janet is a single Mom who is enjoying the peace and quiet while cooking dinner in the kitchen. Maddie starts humming to herself. After a few seconds, Joey asks her to stop. She says she won't. The bickering escalates.

"Joey, Maddie, that's 1," says Mom.

Both children are now on a count of 1, according to the usual sibling rivalry and counting procedure. In this situation, however, if the kids hit 3, Mom has decided that she will use a unique form of a time-out alternative that is also a natural consequence (see Chapter 13). The bickering continues through a count of two, so at 3 Mom says:

"OK, guys. That's 3, separate."

This means that the children have to go to different places. They cannot be together. It's like the old bar-closing adage: "You don't have to go to your room, but you can't stay here." Both kids must leave the room they were sharing. Where they go is their choice, except that they cannot choose the same place. They may bring their toys.

Comment: Good creativity by this mother. Separate here is more of an interruption or redirection than a punishment. Separate can also be useful if the kids share a room and can't both go there for time-out. And the separation period can last the usual one minute per year, or it can be longer—until dinner is served, for instance. If the kids don't comply, the usual time-out is in order.

Arguing

As Mom is working in the kitchen after dinner, eleven-year-old Jeff asks:

"Can I go out after dinner to play?"
"No, dear, you still have homework to do," says Mom.
"I'll do it when I come back in, right before bed."
"That's what you said last night, honey, and it didn't work. Remember?"
"Oh, please Mom. I promise!" (Badgering, Butter Up)
"Get your homework done first, and then you can go out. If you work hard, it shouldn't take more than a half-hour."
"Why can't I just go out now!? I'll DO MY STUPID HOMEWORK!" (Intimidation)
"That's 1."
"I can't wait to grow up so I can go in the army. It's got to be more fun than living in this dump." (Martyrdom)
"That's 2."
"All right, all right, all right." (Jeff goes to start his homework.)

Comment: Mom did very well here. She tried a little negotiating, but when that didn't work she didn't get caught up in a useless argument or try to explain why her house wasn't the same as the military.

Sibling Rivalry II

Sean, 9, and Tammi, 11, are getting into it while trying to play Scrabble in the living room. Dad is washing dishes in the kitchen.

"It's my turn."

"No it isn't. You lost it 'cause you took so long."

"Give me that. I was going to pick up that one!"

"You scratched me!"

"I did not, you idiot! You started it!"

"You're so dumb it isn't funny."

Dad enters. "What's going on here?"

"She's cheating!"

"I am not, lamebrain. You're too slow!"

"Be quiet, both of you! Tell me what happened."

General yelling and chaos follow the ill-fated inquiry.

"OK, that's 1 for both of you."

General yelling and chaos continue.

"That's 2."

Sean dumps the Scrabble board over, grabs a bunch of letters, and throws them at the piano.

"Sean, that's 3, take a rest for 10."

Comment: Dad recovered pretty well after asking the world's dumbest question. He should have started counting earlier.

Extreme Possessiveness

Haley is four years old. She has a playdate—at her own house—with another little girl, Alyssa, whom she has just met. Unfortunately, everything Alyssa touches, Haley tries to take away from her. Alyssa is not aggressive at all, but just stands there looking bewildered after a new toy has been taken from her hands.

Mom sees the pattern. Alyssa picks up a small red car. Haley moves in and grabs it. Mom says:

"Haley, that's 1. You must let Alyssa play with something."

Haley still doesn't let go."

"Haley, that's 2."

The little girl releases her hold and lets Alyssa have the car.

"That's very nice of you, sweetheart."

Comment: Good job. Explain, count and praise cooperation.

Conclusion

What have our tales from the trenches taught us? Kids can certainly catch you off guard, for one thing! You have to be on your toes and—to be fair to yourself and the children—you have to make reasonable and fairly rapid decisions about what is countable and what is not. Good counting takes a little bit of practice, but once you master the skill, you'll wonder how you ever got along without this sanity-saving technique.

CHAPTER SUMMARY

Is It Magic?

The "magic" of the 1-2-3 procedure is not in the counting itself. The power of the method comes primarily from your ability to accomplish two goals. Your first objective is to explain—when necessary—and then keep quiet. Your second objective is to count as calmly and unemotionally as you can.

Do these two things well and your children will start listening to you!

12
More Serious Offenses in Tweens

An ounce of prevention is worth a pound of cure.

A new type of human being has invaded the planet. It's called a "tween." A tween, supposedly, is a nine-to-twelve-year-old who is already experiencing distinct adolescent tendencies. These days parents swear that their eight-year-olds are already acting like teenagers!

Can you still use *1-2-3 Magic* with these tween creatures? Certainly. Counting and your other two parenting jobs still apply. In fact, all three of your parenting jobs are even more important as your kids approach their adolescent years.

Some tweens, though, may present a unique problem. They may do things that fall into the category of Stop behavior, but their actions are too serious for our counting and time-out procedures. Included in this worrisome list of childhood exploits are lying, stealing, physical fights, cutting school, behavioral problems during school, bullying, property damage, pranks, not coming home, staying out late, smoking and starting fires. Stronger—but non-abusive—action is now required on a parent's part. You want to make sure your kids do not repeat these more troublesome activities, but you also don't want to start a war with your own offspring.

When tweens commit more serious offenses, your goal should be this: *Preventing future behavior problems while at the same time maintaining a good parent/child relationship.* It's all too easy—when you're mad and scared—to jump into the demanding/firm side of parenting and totally forget the warm/friendly side. Having an angry policeman for a parent is a very dangerous way for your sons and daughters to start their adolescent careers.

Quik Tip

More serious misbehavior by tweens can be both aggravating as well as scary. And when that happens, it's very easy for parents to jump into the angry policeman role and forget the warm/friendly relationship part of the parenting equation. That's a dangerous way for your kids to start adolescence.

Some normal pre-adolescent children, especially boys, engage in isolated incidents that include the unusual and harmful activities listed above. Sometimes these kids are influenced by other children to do things they wouldn't otherwise do. Exercising temporary poor judgment, these youngsters are going along for the ride. When parents respond with a firm hand and a fair punishment, these first-time offenders do not become repeat offenders. This chapter will help you deal with such children and such incidents.

Other times, however, the trouble-producing motivation comes from inside the child himself. When a child starts showing a pattern of unusually hostile, aggressive, rule-breaking behavior, we begin to worry—especially as the youngster gets older. That's why we are so interested in early prevention: The older they are, the harder kids are to change. This chapter will help you manage more upsetting childhood behavior reasonably, firmly and calmly.

Most parents will not need to use this chapter a lot—or perhaps even at all. But when it is necessary, the kind of targeted, rational management described here is essential in preventing the problem behavior of vulnerable, higher-risk children from escalating as they grow up.

Oppositional Defiance and Conduct Disorder

Although we do not totally understand why some tweens start down a destructive path of behavior, we do know a few things. Two motives that have been implicated in the more serious behavioral problems listed before are 1) hostile and vengeful inclinations and 2) thrill-seeking.

Hostile or vengeful impulses, for example, may drive behavior such as fighting, bullying and damaging property. Thrill-seeking may be involved in smoking, cutting school and starting fires. Many problem behaviors, of course, can involve both motives. When this is the case, the reinforcement a young lad gets from engaging in a "double-motive" activity can be even more powerful and dangerous.

Adolescents and preteens who consistently engage in aggressive, destructive, rule-breaking behavior that hurts others or damages property are often diagnosed with Conduct Disorder (CD). Their troublesome activities often reflect the two motives of hostile aggression and thrill-seeking. These CD children also often have problems with learning disabilities, attention deficit disorder, language and communication, and the ability to read social cues. As you may have guessed, Conduct Disorder is the modern euphemism for juvenile delinquency.

Young kids and tweens who sometimes seem to get addicted to hostile and vengeful behavior are often referred to as Oppositional Defiant Disorder (ODD) children. While CD youths may want to hurt you, ODD kids simply like to aggravate you. ODD kids are negative, defiant and can't take no for answer. They deliberately annoy other people, are in turn easily annoyed themselves, and blame everybody else for anything that goes wrong. ODD kids are Super Brats, and they are no fun to live with.

ODD probably has some genetic basis, but this disorder can also be caused—as well as seriously aggravated—by sloppy, inconsistent, angry and overly wordy parenting. In any case, ODD behavior starts at home. And when poor parenting is part of the picture, Oppositional Defiant kids can graduate to become Conduct Disorder kids; they simply take their troublesome behavior out of the house and into the community. CD teens are dangerous kids with treacherous futures.

One of the goals of *1-2-3 Magic* is to prevent oppositional defiance from starting in the first place by means of reasonable, gentle and solid parenting. A second goal of *1-2-3 Magic* is to eliminate early ODD behavior problems—once they have started—so they don't change into Conduct Disorder. Get rid of early ODD and you cut the risk of later trouble tremendously.

For most parents, who don't have kids who are at risk for major Oppositional Defiant problems, the basic *1-2-3 Magic* program will be sufficient. With higher-risk tweens who start engaging in more serious problem behavior, parents will need to pay particular attention to what we call the Major/Minor System.

The Major/Minor System

Your next door neighbor rings your front door bell on a beautiful summer day. This fellow has never been the most pleasant person in the world, but today he is furious. He informs you that your nine-year-old son, Doug, just put a rock through his garage window. Deliberately. Your neighbor wants to know what you're going to do about it and how you're going to punish the kid.

You are shocked, embarrassed and incredulous. You apologize to the aggravated man and tell him you'll certainly take care of it. Doug isn't a nasty problem child, but you know he's had a few run-ins with this guy, who does tend to be a real grouch sometimes. If your boy did throw a rock through the neighbor's garage window, that would obviously be Stop behavior, but it wouldn't make much sense to run to the back door and say, "Doug, that's 1." "That's 3, take 5 and add 15 for the seriousness of the offense" would also seem too mild. Some punishment may be called for, but even then, you still want to avoid a lot of the excess talking and emotion that will only make things worse.

Fortunately, there is a very simple punishment system that you can set up to handle serious problems like this with a minimum of upset and confusion. It's called the Major/Minor System. With the Major/Minor System you will establish appropriate Major or Minor punishments/consequences for corresponding Major or Minor offenses. The Major/Minor System is applied differently depending upon how much trouble you've had in the past with your child. Is this the first time that you've had a serious problem with this child, or have there been repeated episodes?

The Major/Minor System for First-Time Offenses

With first-time offenses, like Doug in our example above, you only need to deal with the problem at hand. You do not need to make a big list of behavior and punishments like you may do with repeated problems.

So let's imagine that after your irate neighbor leaves, you track down Doug. You tell him about your conversation with Mr. Antagonisky from next door. Then you ask your son what happened. You remain calm and "put on your sympathetic listening shoes" (see Chapter 19). Doug is not a bad kid, and you're determined to hear him out first, then determine what needs to be done.

Doug tells you that he was playing catch in the backyard with his friend, Chris. They were using a tennis ball. At one point Doug missed Chris' throw and it went into Antagonisky's yard, where Mr. A. was tending his flowers. Doug retrieved the ball, but while doing so, he accidentally stepped on one of Mr. A.'s stupid plants. Doug said that the guy then went ballistic, screaming and swearing at both boys and also looking physically threatening. In frustration as well as anger—and also not wanting to look scared—Doug had turned around and thrown the ball in the general direction of the neighbor's garage. He wasn't aiming at the small window, he said, but he did hear the sound of shattering glass.

How should you apply the Major/Minor System? Tell your son that even though Mr. A. is not the most diplomatic person in the world, Doug exercised poor judgment during the incident by letting his own temper get the best of him and throwing the ball at the garage. Doug therefore is going to have to accept several consequences, and the consequences here will not involve time-out. First, the boy will go back and tell Antagonisky that he, Doug, will clean up the glass in the garage and pay for a replacement pane and the installation costs. Doug will also ask Mr. A. if he would like the plant replaced, and pay for that if necessary. You tell Doug that he can apologize if he so desires, but even if he doesn't, he must be polite and civil during the conversation—even if Antagonisky is not.

This punishment constitutes a major consequence for your son. Your assignment will be no small chore for the young lad. Doug does as instructed, though, and the problem is resolved. You tell your boy you're proud of him and the way he handled the situation. No other consequences—or lectures—are necessary.

By the way, you, the parent here, also did a good job. You did not beat down your son because you were embarrassed, nor did you let your boy off the hook because of your dislike for your next door neighbor.

The Major/Minor System for Repeat Offenses

What if, on the other hand, you've had a number of more serious problems with your ten-year-old son, Mike? In the last several months, Mike's been late to school three times (you think maybe on purpose) and come home in the evening more than an hour late twice. You also think he smells like he's been smoking a few times, he's been carrying matches, and you're never sure if he's lying about doing his homework. Mike's grades have slipped from a B+ to a C+ average in the last two quarters, and you really don't care for one of his new friends. Your son also seems less communicative.

Quik Tip
Remember that—even with more serious offenses—fits of temper and righteous indignation from you can ruin the effectiveness of whatever punishments or consequences are chosen. You need to be decisive *and* calm.

When kids start acting up like this, it's easy to get so irritated so often that all you can think of is doling out punishment. When a child does something right, you ignore the good deed and think, "Well, it's about time!" When he does something wrong, however, you angrily jump all over him. This defensive and aggressive stance on your part runs the risk of making the child so angry that he is more likely to engage in vengeful and hostile—as well as perhaps thrill-seeking—behavior, and the reaction and counterreaction sequence can be the start of a domestic war, with the result that your child's future is in great jeopardy.

Instead of that unproductive, knee-jerk type of parenting, your strategy with Mike should involve two primary lines of attack: 1) improving your relationship with your boy through regular doses of praise, one-on-one shared fun, and sympathetic listening and 2) close but reasonable supervision using the Major/Minor System.

We'll discuss how to improve a relationship with a child more specifically in Part V. Here we'll focus on the Major/Minor System. You will set up a well-defined system of behavioral consequences for Mike. The consequences or punishments will depend on the seriousness of the behavior involved, varying from major offenses to minor transgressions (minor offenses here are still more serious than countable problems). Actually, it's usually helpful to have a three-level, Major/Medium/Minor list of consequences that include variations of groundings, fines, chores, community service or educational activities. For example:

Major Consequences

> *Grounding:* two weeks restriction to room after dinner and on weekends; no electronic entertainment (TV, computer, games) or phone
>
> *Fine:* $25 or pay back double the value of stolen or damaged articles
>
> *Chores:* 15 hours work around the house
>
> *Community service:* 15 hours volunteer work at church or other institution
>
> *Educational activity:* research subject (e.g., smoking) and write quality eight-page paper, attend group counseling

Medium Consequences

> *Grounding:* one-week restriction to room after dinner and on weekends; no electronic entertainment (TV, computer, games) or phone
>
> *Fine:* $10 or pay back double the value of stolen or damaged articles
>
> *Chores:* eight hours work around the house
>
> *Community service:* eight hours volunteer work at church or other institution
>
> *Educational activity:* research subject (e.g., smoking) and write quality four-page paper

Minor Consequences

> *Grounding:* two day restriction to room after dinner; no electronic entertainment (TV, computer, games) or phone
>
> *Fine:* $5 or pay back double the value of stolen or damaged articles
>
> *Chores:* four hours work around the house
>
> *Community service:* four hours volunteer work at church or other institution
>
> *Educational activity:* research subject (e.g., smoking) and write quality two-page paper

The punishments for Major offenses are greater than the punishments for Medium ones, and Medium consequences are bigger than those for Minor problems. The above ideas are only suggestions: These guidelines will certainly be altered by individual families. (Over the years I have learned that *there will always be* some people who think I am too strict, and others who think I am not strict enough!) Again, keep in mind that even the Minor offenses described in this chapter are still more serious than countable things such as arguing, yelling, teasing, whining and so on.

Once you have come up with your punishment classifications, you decide which behavior merits which class of punishment. When that misbehavior occurs, one of the consequences from the list is implemented (not the whole list!). This process saves a lot of effort and deliberation, and also lets your youngster know the consequences beforehand if he decides to mess up. Some parents even let the child pick the consequence—once the Major, Medium or Minor category has been chosen.

Recall that your son Mike was acting up more in the last few months. With Mike you work out the following classifications:

Major Offenses

Coming home more than two hours late
Playing with or starting any fire without parent present

Medium Offenses

Coming home one to two hours late
Getting to school more than five minutes late
Lying about more serious matters
Carrying matches or lighter

Minor Offenses

Coming home up to one hour late
Getting to school less than five minutes late
Lying about homework

Once the system is set up, when Mike pulls a fast one, you simply categorize it and determine the consequence. No yelling or screaming by you is allowed, of course, though a *short* explanation or discussion may occasionally be in order (see Chapter 21). What if the youngster does something that you didn't put on the original Major/Minor list? You just classify it as Major, Medium or Minor and then pick a punishment.

You can adjust the Major/Minor System after you set it up, but be careful not to make punishments so harsh that they backfire. One family, I remember, had a Major/Minor System in place, like the one described above, for their twelve-year-old son. Then one day they found out that the boy had stolen a bike. The major punishments suddenly didn't seem like strong enough consequences for this act, so they told the boy he was grounded for a year! Discipline like this will never work because it will be impossible to enforce and it will probably start a war. A better punishment would have been a grounding for a month and a requirement to pay back the value of the bike.

Quik Tip

When using the Major/Minor System, make sure the consequences aren't so harsh that they backfire. And build in some kind of reward for a child's going a number of days or weeks without any problem at all. That's an accomplishment that should be recognized!

If you've been having a serious problem with repeated offenses, you can also make a chart that keeps track of the number of days in a row in which the child stays free of trouble. There might even be a reward for this good performance, such as a special outing with one parent (not with the whole family!). If serious problems continue in spite of the Major/Minor System—and in spite of your working to improve the relationship with the youngster—it is time for an evaluation with a professional.

Several other prevention-oriented thoughts are in order here. If you have a young lad who seems inclined along ODD/CD lines, research has shown that there are a number of important factors that can help prevent future problems. And these factors are—at least to some extent—under parental control. These problem-reducing forces include day-to-day discipline consistency, consistency between parents, marital stability, parental mental health and close—but reasonable—supervision of the child. A huge *problem-increasing* force is parental drug and alcohol use. Don't play around with an ODD/CD-type child. They are time bombs.

Lying

The problem of children lying is included in this chapter for two reasons: 1) lying itself is a more serious offense and 2) lying is often used to cover up other serious offenses. Lying drives some parents crazy, and managing this problem is often confusing and difficult. Therefore we'll try to provide some basic guidelines.

There are basically two kinds of lies. The first kind involves making up stories that are designed to impress other people and build up one's ego. This type of verbal fabrication is not common in children. The second—and by far the most common type—is lying to avoid trouble. This type may involve covering up a past misdeed or trying to get out of some unpleasant task. Kids who steal, for example, will almost always lie about the theft when they are initially confronted. Other kids lie about not having homework so they won't have to face that boring job.

When it comes to dealing with lying, parents, first of all, should remember not to treat the act as if it were the equivalent of homicide, grand larceny or adultery. Not telling the truth certainly isn't a good thing, but it's not usually a truly terrible behavior. Many parents get so upset about lying that they act as though the world were coming to an end. These upset grownups accomplish two things: 1) they lead the child to believe that he is a horrible person, and 2) they increase the probability of more lies in the future.

What Should You Do About Lying?

The school calls on Tuesday at 1 p.m. to tell you that your ten-year-old son, Tom, got into a fight with a boy named Davey Smith at lunchtime. At 3:45 Tom comes home. Mom starts the conversation like this:

"How was your day?"
"Good. You made me my favorite sandwich for lunch."
"Speaking of lunchtime, how did that go?"
"Fine, we played some baseball."
"Anything unusual happen?
"No."
"OK, listen, young man. You're lying to me. I got a call from the school today and Mr. Pasquini told me you got into a fight with ... etc., etc."

In this conversation the parent is "cornering" the youngster. Sure, this parent wants to get some information from her son, but *first* Mom wants to *test* the boy to see if he'll tell the truth. Is this the right way to handle the situation? The answer is no.

When you know some kind of trouble has occurred, a primary rule is this: Don't corner children. Imagine that one night right after dinner you give your child the third degree about whether or not he has homework. He denies having any homework six times and then finally, after your seventh question, he breaks down and admits that he has some math to do. By this time, of course, you are furious, but you also feel victorious that you finally got the truth out of the kid.

But what has really just happened? You have given your child six times to practice lying! You may think to yourself, "Sooner or later he'll realize he can't fool me and he'll give up." Sometimes kids will give up, but many children will continue trying to take the easy way out first. They will simply work to become better liars and you will be helping to provide them with their practice sessions.

Here's a more constructive approach. Imagine something bad has happened. You either know the truth or you don't. If you don't know what occurred, ask the youngster once what happened. If he tells you the story and you find out later that the child lied, punish him for whatever the offense was as well as for the lie, using the Major/Minor System.

Try not to surprise the child by asking your question on the spur of the moment. Many kids simply respond impulsively. They lie, but their real desire is just to end the conversation, get rid of you and stay out of trouble.

What if something bad has happened and you already know all the gory details? You might say something like this: "I want you to tell me the story of what happened at lunch today, but not right now. Think about it a while and we'll talk in fifteen minutes. But remember I already talked with Mr. Pasquini." No lectures or tantrums from you.

There is another option many parents use when 1) they already know what happened and 2) the child is very likely to lie about the event no matter how the questions are phrased. In this case you simply tell the youngster what you know and then calmly mete out the punishment. You do not even give the child the chance to lie. Under these circumstances many kids will blow up and accuse you of not trusting them (Testing Tactic #2, temper). Manage the testing by ignoring their statement or counting them, and end the conversation with, "I'm sure you'll do better next time."

When you have a child who uses lying regularly to avoid unpleasant tasks, such as chores or homework, try to fix the problem—as much as you can—so that lying does not seem necessary to the child. If your son continually lies about homework, for example, work out some kind of communication with the teacher, such as a daily assignment sheet. Then use the tactics described in Chapter 17, such as the PNP routine and Rough Checkout. For chores, consider fixing the problem by the judicious use of other Start behavior strategies (see Chapter 13).

Lying is not good, but it certainly isn't the end of the world either. Most people, children as well as adults, probably tell a few "stretchers" from time to time. Not telling the truth doesn't mean that your kids don't love you or that they are bound to grow up to become inmates in a federal penitentiary. Lying is a problem, though, and it needs to be managed carefully and thoughtfully. Over the years, frequent emotional overreactions from you—combined with badgering and cornering—can help produce an Accomplished Liar.

Congratulations! You have just learned Parenting Job #1: Controlling Obnoxious Behavior. You are ready to begin counting, and you are prepared for testing and manipulation from your kids. So now we're on to the next giant parenting job: Encouraging Good Behavior.

Part IV
Encouraging Good Behavior
(Job #2)

Chapter 13
Establishing Positive Routines

Chapter 14
Up and Out in the Morning

Chapter 15
Cleaning Up and Chores

Chapter 16
Suppertime

Chapter 17
Homework

Chapter 18
Going to Bed – And Staying There!

13
Establishing Positive Routines

Scientists discover room-cleaning gene on chromosome 11!

Now we turn our attention to your second big parenting job: encouraging your children *to* do the positive things you want them to do. We call this behavior category Start behavior, because you want your children to *start* doing their schoolwork, going to bed, eating their supper, cleaning their rooms and getting up and out in the morning.

Recall that Start behavior requires more motivation from children than Stop behavior. While it may only take one second to stop whining or arguing, tasks such as doing homework or getting up and off to school may require thirty minutes or more. Kids not only have to start these jobs, they also have to continue and finish them. Counting difficult behavior is fairly easy. When it comes to positive behavior, however, moms and dads have to be more skilled motivators.

Many parents, when beginning 1-2-3 Magic, use counting first for a week to ten days before tackling Start behavior. If you try to do the whole program at once (both Stop and Start problems), it may be confusing or take too much energy. Equally important, it will also be a lot easier to get the kids to do the good things if they know you have gotten back in control of the house by effectively managing their obnoxious conduct.

When you begin using your Start behavior tactics, don't be surprised if you run into testing and manipulation. Your daughter may not thank you for training her to clean her room. If you have worked on counting negative behavior first, you will have had a fair amount of experience in dealing with Stop behavior, such as testing, before you tackle the task of getting the kids to do the good things. So have your counting strategy ready in your back pocket.

Quik Tip
With Start behavior, you can use more than one tactic at a time for a particular problem. You may even come up with some of your own strategies. Remember: Train the kids to do what you want, or keep quiet!

When dealing with Start behavior, keep in mind one of the basic rules of *1-2-3 Magic*: *Train the children or keep quiet!* In the 1-2-3 program there is a method for handling just about every kind of problem your kids can throw at you. So use these methods! Kids, for example, are not born to be natural room cleaners. If the child isn't cleaning his room, train him to clean it. Otherwise, be quiet, clean it yourself or close the door and don't look. Training, however, does not mean nagging, arguing, yelling or hitting.

Wonderful, Powerful Routines!

Many people think the word "routine" means bad and boring. You will soon learn, however, that when it comes to Start behavior, routines are wonderful and powerful. Activities like homework and going to bed are complex and take time. Kids have to learn to regularly follow a fixed sequence of actions. Same time, same place, same way. Once a routine is mastered, kids tend to do it automatically.

Routines for positive behavior, therefore, drastically reduce your discipline problems and they can also make testing and manipulation virtually nonexistent. The first two steps in establishing a routine, which we'll discuss at the end of this chapter, are:

1. Define the procedure for the kids
2. Rehearse the procedure with the kids

There are seven Start behavior tactics you can consider using to establish and maintain your routines. Sometimes you may use just one tactic, but other times you may use two or three for the same problem. While counting obnoxious behavior is fairly straightforward, you can be more creative and flexible when managing positive behavior. In fact, many parents and teachers have come up with useful and imaginative ideas that are not on our list.

Here are our seven strategies for encouraging good behavior:

1. Praise (Positive Reinforcement)
2. Simple Requests
3. Kitchen Timers
4. The Docking System
5. Natural Consequences
6. Charting
7. Counting Variation

With these rules in mind, let's take a look at the seven tactics you will use to get the kids to do what they're supposed to.

1. Praise (Positive Reinforcement)

Why is there a "home-field advantage" in sports? It's because the crowd encourages their team by cheering and applauding. Even for adult professional athletes, this type of praise is a strong motivator. Unfortunately, however, this home-field-advantage effect doesn't always translate from stadium to home. Why?

Angry people make noise; happy people keep quiet. That's why. We all suffer from a biological curse that motivates us to say something to our kids when we're angry at them, but to keep quiet when the little ones are doing what we want them to do. Imagine it's a Sunday in October and I'm watching a football game in the afternoon. My two children are in the next room playing a game with each other, having a great time and getting along very well. What do you think the chances are that I'm going to get up out of my chair, walk all the way into the next room, and say, "Gee, I'm delighted you guys are having such a good time!"? That would be a great thing, but the chances of my doing it are about zero. Why? Because when adults are happy and content themselves, they are not particularly motivated to do anything more than what they're already doing.

But imagine that my children in the next room start fighting and screaming. Why do they behave this way?! I can't even hear the football game!! Now I am motivated—I'm mad. Now the chances of my getting up, running into the other room and yelling at the kids to keep quiet are high. Anger is a much better motivator than contentment. The result is that our kids are more likely to hear from us when we have negative rather than positive feedback. Youngsters as well as spouses can start feeling they're just a pain in the neck to us.

One powerful antidote to our unfortunate biological orientation is praise, or positive verbal reinforcement. As the saying goes about voting in Chicago, praise should be done early and often. Your praise and other positive interactions with your kids should outnumber your negative comments by a ratio of about three or four to one. If you look, you shouldn't have trouble finding something to reinforce:

"Thanks for doing the dishes."
"You started your homework all by yourself!"
"That dog really likes you."
"You kids did a good job of getting along during the movie."
"I think you got ready for school in record time this morning!"
"Good job on that math test, John."
"I saw you out on the soccer field. You played hard—good hustle!"
"That's wonderful! I can't believe it! How on earth did you
   do that?!"

Once you've gotten the kids successfully carrying out a particular Start behavior routine, praise can help keep the cooperation or good performance going. Many parents, for example, praise or thank their kids for complying with simple requests or for following a bedtime or homework routine.

Keep a sensitive eye on your son or daughter, though, because praise should be tailored to some extent to each child. Some kids like rather elaborate, syrupy and emotional verbal reinforcement, while others do not. Your eight-year-old daughter, for instance, gets 100 percent on Wednesday on her spelling pretest. You say, "Oh Melissa, that's just marvelous! I can't believe it! We're going to frame this paper and also fax it to grandma in Florida!!" Melissa eats it up. Melissa's eleven-year-old brother, however, would be nauseated by that kind of talk. For him, "Good job—keep up the good work," and a pat on the shoulder might be enough. Your job is to praise the child, not to embarrass him.

The tactic of praise sometimes gets criticized for being overused and abused. People say we spoil our children with exaggerated compliments, artificially inflate their self-esteem, and consequently don't prepare them for the big, bad world. Is this a real problem?

Here's the deal. With kids up to age about five or six, it's not so bad to exaggerate your praise of their effort or their performance. They respond positively to almost any kind of encouragement *and they don't always really know how well or poorly they are doing*. But watch out when those kids hit first or second grade! Now they are starting to get an idea of what doing well really means, and they will increasingly be able to tell fake from genuine praise.

> **Quik Tip**
>
> Are we spoiling our kids with superficial, phoney praise? First and second graders are starting to get an idea of what good effort and good performance really mean. More and more they will be able to tell fake from genuine praise.

There are two additional devices you can use to make praise a more effective boost to a child's self-esteem: 1) *praise in front of other people* and 2) *unexpected praise*. While you're talking to your next door neighbor, for example, your daughter Kelsey shows up. You interrupt your conversation and say, "You should have seen Kelsey out there on the soccer field today. Those other kids never knew what hit them!" Kelsey will beam with pride.

Unexpected praise can also be quite memorable for a child. Your son is upstairs doing his homework. You call from the bottom of the stairs, "Hey, Jordan!" Jordan has no idea what's coming next. You then say, "Did I tell you what a great job you did on the yard?" Jordan will be pleased—and perhaps a little relieved!

How do you keep offering praise and encouragement on a regular basis? As mentioned before, this task is surprisingly difficult, since most of us tend to shut up when we are content. Here are two suggestions. First, see if you can make two or three positive comments for every one negative comment (and, by the way, a count is one negative comment). These positive remarks don't have to be made at the same time, of course. They can be made later. If the two-or-three-to-one ratio idea doesn't appeal to you, a second strategy is to have a quota system. Each day you make a deal with yourself that you will make at least five positive comments to each child (consider doing the same with your spouse).

Make sure your kids get the home-field advantage!

2. Simple Requests

The problem with simple requests is that they are not so simple. Parental requests to children can be made more or less effective by the parent's tone of voice, the spontaneity of the request and the phrasing of the demand.

We all have different *voices*. When she was younger, my daughter had several different variations of the simple expression, "Dad!" One "Dad!" meant I'm excited and want to show you something. Another "Dad!" meant I want assistance because my brother is teasing me. And yet a third "Dad!" (during her teen years) meant, "Cool it, oldtimer, you're embarrassing me in public!"

Parents have different voices too; the voice we're concerned about here is called "chorevoice." Chorevoice has a quality of "You're not

doing what I expect and it's really irritating and what's the matter with you and when are you going to learn ..." etc., etc. Chorevoice has an aggravated, nagging and anxious tone that most children find aggravating. When this parental tone of voice is coupled with a request, therefore, it makes cooperation less likely because you are now asking an angry child to cooperate.

A good antidote to chorevoice is a businesslike, matter-of-fact presentation. "John, it is now time to start your homework" or "Taylor, bedtime." This tone of voice implies, "You may not like this but it's got to be done now." Testing is much less likely when requests are made in a matter-of-fact way, but—believe it or not—the mere tone of voice can also say, "If you test or push me, you'll get counted."

The *spontaneity* of a parental request can also be a cooperation killer. Your son is outside playing baseball with some friends. You go to the front door and ask him if he'd come in and take out the garbage. He blows his stack and you think, "What is the big deal?" You are correct that your boy overreacted, but the big deal was not the garbage. The big deal to him was the spontaneity. What do you expect the youngster to say? "Thanks for offering me this opportunity to be of service to the family"?

No one likes spur-of-the-moment interruptions that involve unpleasant tasks. You don't like them either, but you are often stuck with such intrusions. But we're not talking about getting you to cooperate here, we're talking about getting your kids to cooperate. And we're also not saying your children shouldn't have chores to do. They *should* help out around the house. The point is this: Structure these tasks into fixed routines so that spontaneous requests are seldom necessary.

Finally, the *phrasing* of a request can make a difference in how kids respond. Phrasing a request as a question and adding the ridiculous "we" to the statement will often ensure noncompliance or testing and manipulation. A super-sweet "Don't we think it's about time to start our homework?" for example, is almost guaranteed to elicit a negative response. "I want your schoolwork complete by five o'clock" is better.

What if, in spite of everything, your simple request still does no good? We'll come back to that question at the end of this chapter after we've discussed several other Start behavior options.

3. Kitchen Timers

Kitchen timers are wonderful devices for encouraging good behavior in children. Many kinds are useful, including the sixty-minute wind-up variety as well as computer, small LCD and even hourglass varieties. The people who manufacture timers think they're for baking cakes. They're not—timers are for raising kids! Kitchen timers can be a great help for just about any Start behavior routine, whether it's picking up, feeding the fish, getting up in the morning, taking the garbage out or go-

ing to bed. Kids, especially the younger ones, have a natural tendency to want to beat a ticking mechanical device. The problem then becomes a case of man against machine (rather than child against parent).

These portable motivational gadgets can also be used, if you like, to time the time-outs themselves. Many kids actually prefer doing the time-out with a timer.

You can also take timers in the car with you and use them—as we'll see later—to help control sibling rivalry. Timers can be part of routines for bedtime or bath time or getting up and out in the morning.

Timers also can soften the blow of unavoidable spontaneous requests. A friend of yours calls and says she'll be over in fifteen minutes. You say to your five-year-old daughter, "You've got three things in the kitchen I would like picked up and put in your room. I'm setting the timer for ten minutes and I'll bet you can't beat it!"

Her response will often be, "Oh yes I can!" and the youngster will be hurrying off to do the job. You could take this same approach to get an eleven-year-old to pick up, but you would phrase your request in a more matter-of-fact manner. If the child doesn't respond before the timer dings, you can use the Docking System (see strategy #4) or a version of natural consequences (see strategy #5).

Kitchen timers are also effective because they are not testable. Machines cannot be emotionally manipulated. Imagine you had to remind your son to call his grandmother to thank her for the birthday present she mailed. Your son balks, so you set the timer for ten minutes. The boy's response is "This is stupid!" (Testing Tactic #2, temper). Your response is silence. The timer's response is tick, tick, tick.

4. The Docking System

The principle of docking wages is this: If you don't do the work, you don't get paid. The basic idea of the Docking System is similar: If you don't do the work, I'll do it for you and you'll pay me. The Docking System is for children who are kindergarten-age or above.

This plan, of course, requires that the kids first have a source of funds from an allowance, work around the house, birthday gifts or some other financial reservoir. You can consider starting an allowance with children who are about five-years-old or more. The payment doesn't have to be anything large, but it's a good idea to have half of it based on completing jobs around the house (e.g., cleaning the bedroom, chores, homework). The other half is simply given to the child because he is part of the family—and also so you are sure you have some leverage when it comes time to use the Docking procedure.

Let's imagine you've been having discussions with your nine-year-old son about getting a dog. The child wants the dog, but you wisely object that you're concerned he won't feed it properly. Let's assume you get the dog (partly because you want one, too).

You then tell the child what the deal will be. He's nine and gets about $3 per week allowance. You want the dog fed before 6 each night. If he feeds the dog then, fine. If he doesn't get to feeding the dog before 6, you have good news and bad news. The good news is that you will feed the dog for the boy. The bad news is that you charge to feed other people's dogs, and for this mutt it will be 15 cents per feeding taken off your son's $3 allowance. The child readily agrees, since he's so happy about getting the dog to begin with.

Here's how events might play out. The first night you're in the kitchen making dinner, it's 6:10, there's no one around, and the dog's hungry. You wait. At quarter after your son comes running in asking if you fed the dog. You say, "No." He says, "Good!" and he feeds the dog. You praise the boy, "Hey, great job! That dog was sure happy to see you."

The second night you're in the kitchen and it's 6:20. The dog is looking hungry, but you wait. Now it's 6:30 and the dog is licking your legs! So you finally feed the hungry animal. At 6:40 your boy comes running in:

"Did you feed the dog?"
"Yes, I did. I charged you 15 cents from your allowance."
"WELL WHAT DID YOU DO THAT FOR?!" (Yelling)
"That's 1."

This is not a discussion. It *was* a discussion, but now it's an attack. It's simply one version of Testing Tactic #2, temper, and it should be counted. You discuss discussions and you count attacks. In this kind of situation, it's extremely difficult to resist the temptation to get into angry, little-adult types of comments, such as, "Do you remember when we bought this stupid animal for you? What did you say? You said, 'I'll feed the dog every single night. No problem!' Right! Well, here we are on only the second night and I'm already feeding your dog! I'm sick of doing everything around here for all you people!"

What you're saying may be absolutely correct, but tirades like this will do no good. Parental tantrums and righteous indignation will, in fact, cause harm. Your tirade will do two things. First, the outburst will damage your relationship with your child. Second, your blow-up will ruin the effect of the money the boy was docked. So be quiet and let the money do the talking. If money doesn't seem to have much clout with this particular lad, take minutes off TV, game or computer time or use some other reasonable consequence.

> **Quik Tip**
> With the Docking System, you tell the kids, "I have good news and bad news. The good news is that if you forget a chore, I'll do it for you. The bad news is that you're going to pay me for helping you out." Then tell them the exact amount they will have to pay you.

The Docking System is good for lots of things. How many times have you had the feeling that parenting is unfair? About nine million times? This unfairness applies especially to the moms, who often feel they get stuck with all the extra chores around the house. Well, think of this: Now, if you are going to have to do all that stuff, you're going to get paid for it!

Have you ever said to your kids, for example, "I'm happy to do your laundry on Saturday. All you have to do is get your clothes down to the washer by 9. But I'll be darned if I'm going to go up to your room every weekend to get your dirty underwear out from underneath your bed!"

Now let's imagine you're going to use the Docking System for laundry. You say this: "I'm happy to do your laundry on Saturday mornings. All you have to do is get your clothes down to the washer by 9. If you don't get your clothes down by 9, I will go up to your room to get your dirty things. But I charge for that service. And for a pile the size of the one you usually have, it will probably cost you seventy-five cents to a dollar."

5. Natural Consequences

With natural consequences you let the big, bad world teach the child what works and what doesn't. There are times when your staying out of some problems is the best approach. Suppose you have a fourth grader who is taking piano lessons for the first time. She is not practicing as she should,

however, and can't sleep at night because she's worrying that her piano teacher will be mad.

What should you do? Nothing right away. See if the natural consequence of not practicing (teacher's displeasure) will alter your daughter's behavior. Some piano teachers are very good at getting uncooperative kids to tickle the ivories on a regular basis between lessons. If after a few weeks the teacher's efforts don't work, you may want to try other Start behavior tactics, such as using the timer or charting. But leave the situation alone for a while.

Or, suppose you have a boy in the sixth grade. Because you're in a hurry every morning, part of this young fellow's preschool routine is making his own lunch, with goods that you buy, and then brown-bagging it to school. It seems like every other day, though, he is telling you how hungry he was at lunch with nothing to eat. What should you do? Relax, don't lecture, and leave the responsibility squarely on his shoulders. Let the natural consequence (his empty stomach) talk to him instead of his mother talking to him. Give him some encouragement by saying something like this: "I'm sure you'll do better tomorrow."

> **CAUTION**
>
> Natural reinforcers, such as praise, sometimes aren't enough to motivate children to complete a task—especially if the kids hate the job! In these cases artificial rewards can be used; you'll try to borrow some motivation from somewhere else. It works!

Another example of a good time to use natural consequences? The wintertime dress of preteens and adolescents. All parents know that junior high and high school students think there are federal laws against zipping or buttoning up their coats in the winter. These kids do not want to appear as though their mothers dressed them in the morning. The solution? Let the cold talk to the kids if they're not dressed properly, and avoid starting the day with the obvious, aggravating comment, "You're not going out like that again, are you?!"

One final, real-life example of natural consequences: One mother I used to see years ago had a four-and-one-half-year-old boy who was driving her nuts in the morning. The boy was in preschool, but he wouldn't get dressed on time for his car pool ride. Every morning when the horn honked in the driveway, this little guy was sitting in his pajamas watching cartoons on TV. The poor Mom was tearing her hair out.

One morning this mother decided she'd had enough. The boy was in his pajamas watching cartoons when the car in the drive honked. Mom then calmly proceeded to send her son off to school in his pajamas (this was not my idea!). This youngster spent two and one half hours, with his peers, with little flowered booties on and with butterflies all over his chest. At our next session a relieved Mom reported to me that, since that day, she had never again had a problem with her son being ready for his ride.

6. Charting

Charting is a very friendly motivational technique. With charting you use something like a calendar to keep track of how well a child is doing with different Start behavior routines. You can put the chart on the refrigerator door, if public acclaim is desired, or on the back of the child's bedroom door, if privacy is desired. The days of the week usually go across the top of the chart, and down the left side is a list of the tasks the child is working on, such as picking up after herself, getting to bed and clearing the table after supper. If the child completes the task to your satisfaction, you indicate this on the chart with stickers for the little kids (approximate ages four to nine) and grades or points (A-F, 5-1) for the older children.

A typical chart, for example, might have three to five items on it, such as getting up and out, going to bed and taking out the garbage.

With charting, positive reinforcement comes, we hope, from three things: the chart itself, parental praise and the inherent satisfaction of doing a good job. We call these three things *natural* reinforcers. When my daughter was nine, she decided she wanted to take piano lessons. Although this was her choice, she didn't practice regularly and—like the fourth-grader we mentioned earlier—she would worry a lot the night before her lesson that her teacher was going to be upset with her the next day when she couldn't perform well.

We first tried natural consequences, suggesting to our little girl that

	S	M	T	W	T	F	S
UP & OUT		★	★	★			
BEDTIME	★	★	★				
GARBAGE				★			

she work out the problem with her teacher. This tactic failed. So we next tried charting with only natural reinforcers. Our agreement was this: Each day after practicing, our daughter was to find her mother or father and tell that parent exactly how many minutes she had practiced. One of us would then write that number for that day on the chart and praise our budding concert pianist for her work. That was it. The plan worked like a charm.

Unfortunately for us parents, natural reinforcers are frequently insufficient to motivate a child to complete a particular task. Your son, for example, may simply be a natural slob—a clean room means nothing to him. Or your little girl may be attention-deficit and learning-disabled, and homework provides no satisfaction—but much frustration—for her.

In these cases you must use what we call *artificial* reinforcers. Artificial reinforcers mean that the child is going to earn something—which may have nothing directly to do with the task—for successful completion of that task. Since the activity doesn't provide any incentive to the child—and, in fact, may provide a negative incentive—we are going to try to borrow motivation from somewhere else. Our little girl who hates homework, for example, might earn part of her allowance, a special meal or a special time with you.

For smaller children the best ideas are often relatively small things that can be dished out frequently and in little pieces. With older kids, larger rewards that take longer to earn become more feasible. Let yourself be creative in coming up with reinforcers. Rewards certainly do not always have to be material. Some kids, for example, will work hard to earn minutes to stay up later at night, or to be able to do some special activity with one of their parents.

My daughter used what she called a "sticker book" with her three- and five-year-olds. She folded three sheets of colored construction paper together and put two staples in the crease. The child's name then went on the cover along with some decorations. Then she went sticker shopping with the kids and got stickers each of them liked. Whenever the youngster then completed a Start behavior, he or she got to choose a sticker and put it in the book. The kids were proud of their books.

Here is a list of possible artificial reinforcers:

A trip for ice cream	Cash
Brightly colored tokens	Staying up past bedtime
A small toy	Renting a special movie
Renting a special game	A grab-bag surprise
Outing with a parent	Comic book or magazine
Shopping trip	Friend over for supper
Sleepover	Choice of three reinforcers
Playing a game with parent	Reading a story with parent
A "No Chore" voucher	Sleeping with dog or cat
Camping out in backyard	Special phone call
Card for a collection	Other items for collections
Tech time	Helping make and eat cookies
Breakfast in bed	Using power tool with supervision

Keep any chart simple. Three or four things to work on at one time is enough; more than that gets too confusing. I saw a family once who created a chart for their son on which they were attempting to rate thirty-three different behaviors every day! I had to give them an "A" for effort, but also a high rating for confusion.

Keep in mind that you probably will not want to do charting for long periods of time. Charting can become a semi-obnoxious behavioral accounting task, and the positive effects can fade when Mom and Dad are getting tired of filling the chart out every day. So build in "discontinuation criteria"—rules for determining when the chart is no longer necessary.

You might say, for example, that if the child gets good scores (define this precisely) for two weeks running on a particular behavior, that item will be taken off the chart. When the child has earned his way off the chart entirely, it's time to go out for pizza and a movie to celebrate. If after a while the child gets worse again, you can reinstate the chart.

7. Counting Variation: Brief Start Behavior

As mentioned earlier, one of the most frequent mistakes parents make with the 1-2-3 is attempting to use counting to get a child to do Start behavior like homework, chores or getting up and out in the morning. Recall that these tasks can take twenty minutes or more, while counting itself only produces several seconds worth of motivation.

What if the Start behavior itself, however, only required a few seconds worth of cooperation? You want your daughter to hang up her coat, feed the cat or come into the room. Counting, which is so useful for Stop behavior, can be used for some Start behavior, but only on one condition: *What you want the child to do cannot take more than about two minutes.* Your child throws her coat on the floor after school, and you ask her to pick it up. She doesn't, and you say, "That's 1." If she still refuses to comply and gets timed out, she goes and serves the time. When she comes out, you say, "Would you please hang up your coat?" If there is still no cooperation, another time-out would follow.

What if this girl, for some unknown reason, is in a totally ornery mood today and never seems to get the idea? With Start behavior

tactics you have more flexibility. Switch from counting to the Docking System and the kitchen timer. Set the timer for five minutes and tell your daughter she has that time to hang up the coat. If she does pick it up, fine. You promise you'll not say another word. If she doesn't hang the thing up, however, you have good news and bad news. You'll hang up the coat for her, but you will charge for your services. The charge will be twenty-five cents for the coat and twenty-five cents for all the aggravation that was just involved in getting her to hang it up. Keep the talking to a minimum, and count whining, arguing, yelling and other forms of testing.

What can you use this version of the 1-2-3 for? Items like brushing teeth, picking up something, or just "Would you please come here for a second?" You are in the kitchen and you need some help for a minute. You can see your ten-year-old son in the other room, lying on the couch, eyes wide open. You say, "Would you please come here?" His response is "I can't. I'm busy."

This kid's about as busy as a rock. So let's redo this one.

"Would you please come here?"

"I can't. I'm busy."

"That's 1."

"Oh, all right!"

And the reluctant servant enters the room to carry out your bidding.

Simple Requests Revisited

Now let's return to our question about simple requests. What if, in spite of the fact that your voice quality was matter-of-fact, your request was not spur-of-the-moment, and your phrasing was not wishy-washy, your child still does not comply with what you ask him to do? After reading this chapter, you now realize that you have several options.

For example, after your son returned home from school, you told him: "Be sure you change your clothes before you go outside to play." He's been having a snack and playing an electronic game, still in his school clothes, when one of his friends calls him from the back door. Your son calls back that he'll be right out. It doesn't sound as though a different wardrobe is on his mind at all.

Here are some choices you have at this point:

1. Set the *timer* for ten minutes and tell your son, "I want your clothes changed before the timer goes off." Avoid what we call "shouldy" thinking—the kind of parental thinking that expects kids to act like adults. If you were into shouldy thinking, you might have said, "I want your clothes changed before the timer goes off. I already told you that. What does it take to get you to listen to me for once? I'm the one who has to do the laundry, you know, and buy you all sorts of new things to wear!"

   You could also add a *reward* or a *consequence* to the act of changing clothes before the timer goers off. You would not do this every time, but sometimes a strategy like this can "jump-start" the kids into remembering a new behavior. "You change before the timer goes off, you can stay up ten minutes later tonight. If you don't beat the timer, bedtime is ten minutes earlier." Simple, calm, straightforward.

2. Can you use the *Docking System* here? No, because you can't put his clothes on and charge him for the service. You could, of course, use the Docking System if what you had asked your son to do was take out the garbage. After his first refusal of the refuse, you might simply say, "Do you want to take out the trash or do you want to pay me to do it?" Good maneuver.

3. How about *natural consequences* for our reluctant clothes changer? This tactic is a possibility. The boy who plays outside in his school clothes might be required to wash his outfit as soon as he comes in.

4. Finally, you could consider using *counting*. Can your son change clothes in two minutes? Maybe. So as the boy is walking out the door—school outfit still on—you simply say, "That's 1." He probably won't know right away what you're talking about, so he'll respond with, "What?" His comment may even be a little ornery.

   That's good—make him think a little. You pause, then say, "School clothes." If your son then goes off to his room in a huff to change, fine. You probably don't have to count the huff. If, however, he yells at you,

"WHY DO I ALWAYS HAVE TO CHANGE MY IDIOT SCHOOL CLOTHES?! ARE THEY MADE OUT OF GOLD THREADS?!"

Pop quiz: What should you do now?

You got it! You say, "That's 2" for Testing Tactic #2, temper.

Getting Started: Rehearsing Your Routines

It's a good idea to practice the routines once you've defined them. Simply defining a routine and then expecting the kids to comply without any rehearsals is the Little Adult Assumption at work in your brain again. Kids need to *see, feel and remember* how the particular routine works. So make time for some leisurely dress rehearsals of your Start behavior routines—before the procedure actually needs to be used.

With the little ones (under about five) you can use a model-and-pretend method for practicing. You say something like this: "Let's practice getting ready for bed. Isn't that silly, the sun is still shining! What do we have to do to get ready?" Then reinforce the kids' positive answers.

Next you describe the process as you model the procedure for them. "First, I'm going to wash up—just like you said. Then I'm going to put my jammies on (put something over your clothes). Next we sit on the bed for a story."

After you've modeled the routine, have the child do it and praise her (Remember: Some like business and some syrup!) as she goes along: "That's it—you remembered what was next. Good work."

With older kids (five and up), you can skip the modeling by you, and just ask them to go through the motions. Praise the kids and suggest modifications in what they are doing as necessary.

So you rehearse your routines and then start using them. Keep pretty much to same time, same place, same way. But what if at some point the kids get sloppy with their up and out or homework or bedtime? Remember Start behavior tactic #5 on page 127—natural consequences? A natural consequence of getting sloppy with a routine is to rehearse and practice the routine again! No righteous indignation, nagging or arguing from you is necessary. Be nice and praise cooperation. You'll find things will fall back into place.

That's our list of Start behavior strategies. You'll probably be able to come up with several of your own after a while. Next we'll take a look at how to apply these tactics to some of the most common Start behavior problems parents encounter with their youngsters. You're going to be an expert motivator of children in no time!

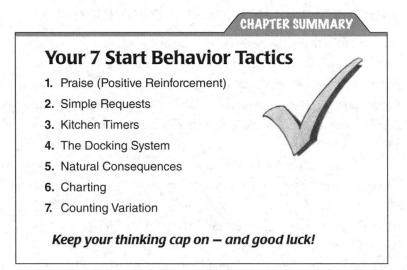

CHAPTER SUMMARY

Your 7 Start Behavior Tactics

1. Praise (Positive Reinforcement)
2. Simple Requests
3. Kitchen Timers
4. The Docking System
5. Natural Consequences
6. Charting
7. Counting Variation

Keep your thinking cap on — and good luck!

14

Up and Out in the Morning

And... they're off!

If ever a routine was sorely needed, it's for this: getting the kids up and out of the house in the morning. Getting up and out is a problem for grammar-school kids, but it can also be an issue for preschoolers, high school students and even spouses. Morning often brings out the worst in everybody. Many people—both parents and kids—are naturally crabby at this point, and there is the additional strain of having to get someplace on time. The pressure, nervousness and emotional thunderstorms that can result have ruined many a parent's day.

For the kids, the morning routine involves a whole sequence of Start behaviors: 1) getting out of bed, 2) bathroom, washing up and brushing teeth, 3) getting dressed, 4) eating breakfast and 5) leaving the house on time with the right equipment. What is required may vary some from family to family (like switching 3 and 4), but it's basically the same job.

Believe it or not, these awful morning situations can often be shaped up rather quickly using some of the Start behavior principles we just outlined. Remember, on schoolday mornings counting will not be your primary tactic. And the No-Talking and No-Emotion rules still apply—even if you haven't had your first cup of coffee.

Before you design your morning routine, a few pieces of advice may help. First, do as much preparation as you can the night before (packing bookbags, selecting clothes, planning breakfast). Second, try to get up fifteen minutes before the kids (older children may give you more snooze time). And third, keep breakfast simple, quick and healthy.

Up and Out for the Little Kids

Very small children in the two-to-five-year-old range are going to need a lot of help and supervision in the morning. These children are not capable of sustaining a positive activity for more than a few minutes, and most of them will not even think of what needs to be done to get out of the house. You're going to have to help two- and three-year-olds get dressed and wash up. Try to do things in the same order each day. You'll also be responsible for remembering anything the children have to take with them. And while you're doing all this, you want to praise lavishly whatever positive efforts they make.

Four- and five-year-olds will often respond to the use of very primitive, basic charts. The chart may have only two or three items on it. These charts can also be combined with kitchen timers to produce an effective motivational system. A chart for a preschooler might look something like this:

	MON	TUES	WED	THURS	FRI
OUT OF BED					
BRUSH TEETH					
GET DRESSED					

Set the timer for fifteen minutes and give the child a cue that it's time to get started. Many of the little ones are already out of bed, so that item on the chart has been successfully completed. Whatever other tasks the youngster finishes before the timer goes off are recognized with special stickers.

With older kids in the primary grades, the chart may have all the morning-routine items on it and the timer may or may not be necessary. For each task, the child earns her favorite sticker for a super job and her next favorite sticker for a good job. No sticker at all means "You blew it today, better luck tomorrow!" The application of the stickers, of course, should be accompanied by a lot of praise: "Good job!" or "Wow, you did it in only twelve minutes!"

In some families, breakfast and TV must wait until the child is totally ready to leave the house—washed, dressed and packed. The breakfast, entertainment and praise serve as reinforcers for the child's successful Start behavior.

What about fighting, teasing, whining or other Stop behavior in the morning? Stop behavior should be counted as usual. If there is time for a time-out, don't hesitate to use time-outs. If there is not enough time, consider using time-out alternatives. "Guys, that's 3. Bedtime is fifteen minutes earlier for both of you tonight. OK, let's get in the car."

Up and Out for Older Kids

For children nine-years-old and up (including high school age), you can still use the methods just described. But if you have the guts—and if you'd like to get out of an unwanted supervisory role faster—here's a version of natural consequences for you. This up-and-out program involves some drastic alterations in the morning routine and these changes will often shock the kids into being much more responsible for themselves. But be forewarned: Extreme self-restraint on the part of moms and dads is required.

Before explaining this new regime, we remind parents that—believe it or not—most kids want to go to school and would be embarrassed if they were late or didn't show up at all. Parents don't realize their children feel this way for two reasons: 1) the kids goof off in the morning instead of getting ready, *but* 2) the kids are able to dilly-dally precisely because their parents have habitually taken *all* the responsibility for their young-sters' making it to school on time.

Now that way of thinking is going to change—in both children and parents. Here's how the new procedure works. You explain to the kids that from now on it will be their responsibility—not yours—to get up and out in the morning. *You will neither supervise them nor nag them.* If you have been waking them up, you will wake them up only once from now on. A better system is to get an alarm clock and show the child how to use it. Explain to the kids that if they go back to sleep after your one wake-up call or after the alarm goes off, you will not wake them again and they will definitely have a problem.

You make it clear to the kids that getting up, getting dressed, washing up, eating breakfast and leaving on time will be their job—totally. If you wish, you can chart the kids on how well they do getting up and out, but, other than casual conversation, you will not say anything to them.

Your children will not believe that you are serious, because they will find it completely incomprehensible that you would ever allow them to get to school late (you may have trouble with that concept, too!). So guess what? You are going to have to make believers out of them.

This new system relies on natural consequences. If the kids dilly-dally in the morning, they are going to run into trouble somewhere. The trouble may be with the other kids in the car pool, who are now afraid that they are going to be late because of your son or daughter (can you stand that?). Or the trouble may come from the child's having to explain to a principal or teacher why he was late and has no parental note excusing him. Most kids don't want these kinds of problems, so we use the threat of these natural consequences to help shape them up.

> **Quik Tip**
>
> Tell your older kids that from now on, getting up and out in the morning is going to be their responsibility—totally. You will neither supervise nor nag them. Your children will not at first believe you are serious, but they *will* believe you are serious after you've let them get burned a few times. What's your chief job in all this? It's keeping quiet.

Some parents can't stand this routine. It drives some grownups crazy to watch their kids fooling around when the bus or car pool ride is coming in five minutes. These are the moments when extreme parental self-restraint is called for. You will want to talk, nag, argue or scream. I've had to ask many parents to take their coffee, retire to the bedroom and not watch the impending disaster. One mother told me, "If I'm going to have to keep quiet and not watch, I want a martini—not a cup of coffee!"

Breakfast is optional for these older children. You can put some food out if that was your usual routine before, but *you can't remind the kids to eat it*. It's better if the kids just get what they want for themselves.

Children won't die from missing breakfast. When they leave, you say nothing about coats, hats or gloves, unless there is danger of frostbite.

What you are doing with this new up-and-out arrangement is teaching the kids responsibility and invoking a sacred rule of psychology: Sometimes Learning the Hard Way is the best way to learn. The lessons sink in more when kids get burned a few times than they do when they simply hear a lecture. So you have to be willing to let the kids get burned. *Don't even start this procedure unless you are convinced you are ready for the strain and—more important—that you can keep quiet.*

It usually takes no more than five days for the child to shape up and successfully get up and out on his own. During that five-day period, your youngster will probably be late to school a few times and will feel embarrassed. He will have had the experience of suddenly realizing at 7:50 that he's not dressed and that Mom didn't remind him that his ride was coming at 8. He may have gotten to school and realized he forgot his math book because he was late leaving. He may also have blown up at his mother a few times (and been counted!) because she didn't provide any reminders or any excuse notes.

Kids have four ways of getting to school: car pool, bus, walking, or riding bikes. When they can walk or bike to school, of course, this up-and-out program is the easiest. With car pools or bus, you can drive the kids if they don't make their connection. Don't rush, however; let them get to school late. Most kids will not get dependent on your driving, especially if they're tardy anyway. If you do have to drive the kids, don't lecture on the way.

These negative experiences have quite an impact on most kids. If the parents are consistent, don't talk and let the kids get burned, the children will shape up in a few days. No "I told you so" comments are allowed. Then things will be much more peaceful at home in the morning and the kids will be much more responsible.

Some parents have used charting along with our natural consequences program. If you decide to do this, make sure you praise good performances ("It's so much easier with you getting yourself up in the morning!") and review the chart at least once a week. You *can* discuss the issue, listen, give brief suggestions or make modifications at times other than when the kids are getting ready in the morning.

Take a Deep Breath

Many parents, before they've used this gutsy procedure, think their kids will be indifferent. Moms and dads think their children really won't care whether or not they get to school on time. Part of the reason the grownups believe this is because the youngsters have said so. Never believe a child who says "I don't care." He usually means the opposite.

If you are skeptical about this up-and-out procedure, consider trying this arrangement and see what happens. Make sure you're ready, though, before you start. Most kids—not all, but most—will shape up. The kids will get up and out on their own. The most important rules are to keep quiet and be willing to let the children get burned—more than once, if necessary. You may want to let the school know what you're doing. Most teachers and principals will cooperate with you, especially if you explain your purpose and label the procedure "independence training."

What if you just don't think you can stand it? Remember that you have some other Start behavior tools for establishing routines. Consider charting, perhaps with artificial reinforcers, and the use of a kitchen timer. Since these kids are older, you might also entertain the idea of discussing your morning routines at a family meeting (see Chapter 22). One way or another, though, it is absolutely critical for everyone to start out the day on a positive note. Adults take bad memories from unsuccessful mornings to work with them, and kids can take those same lousy memories to school.

If you are successful using natural consequences? Relax and enjoy your kids, another cup of coffee, and the peace and quiet. Good luck!

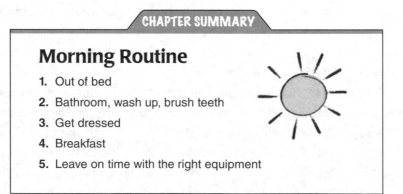

CHAPTER SUMMARY

Morning Routine

1. Out of bed
2. Bathroom, wash up, brush teeth
3. Get dressed
4. Breakfast
5. Leave on time with the right equipment

15
Cleaning Up and Chores

I'll do it later!

While our research over the years has indicated that whining is the most aggravating Stop behavior problem for parents of young children, not cleaning up after yourself has consistently won out as the most irritating Start behavior problem. Some kids leave their stuff strewn all over the house, but amazingly they also have enough left to mess up their entire bedroom. And other undone chores compete with messy houses and messy rooms in the battle to drive parents crazy.

Unfortunately for us, kids are not naturally neat. Many—if not most —in fact, are naturally messy. Perhaps the picking up and chore genes are missing from their chromosomal makeup. Conclusion? The youngsters will have to be _trained_ to pick up, clean their rooms and do chores.

How can you do that? By this time you shouldn't have to be reminded that you won't get the kids to complete these unpleasant tasks by nagging or delivering the lecture, "The Seven Reasons Why It's Easier on Me for You To Have a Clean Room." Counting isn't so helpful either here.

Instead, you have several options for your kids who are four, five and older. Here are some good ones.

Strategies for Cleaning Bedrooms

Your stomach churns with disgust when you view the destruction and chaos that is your daughter's bedroom. Things are thrown all over. You forgot what color the carpet was. The cat was last seen in there three weeks ago. Here a couple of simple routines.

Option 1: Close the Door and Don't Look

Having a clean room is not a life-or-death matter. We know of no research that indicates that kids who didn't keep their rooms neat grow up to be homeless people, mentally unbalanced or more likely to divorce. Besides, whose room is it? You don't have to live in it, so why not just ask the child to keep the door closed so you don't have to be aggravated?

Most parents don't like this idea, but before you dismiss the Close-the-Door-and-Don't-Look method, ask yourself one question: Do you have a child with behavioral or emotional problems, such as ADHD, learning disability, anxiety or depression? If you have a handicapped child or one who's very difficult to begin with, why add another set of difficulties to your problems? Imagine your daughter hates school, hates homework, has no friends, feels lousy most of the time and fights with her brother constantly. Should you also get after her about the stuff lying around on her bedroom floor? You need to straighten out your priorities, because you have bigger fish to fry. Option 1 sure beats yelling and nagging.

Option 1 is quite legitimate for some families, but there are two problems with this procedure: 1) most parents find the notion unacceptable, and 2) dirty dishes and dirty laundry, which can't be ignored.

If you don't want to use Option 1, more suggestions will follow in the next sections of this chapter. As for dirty dishes and dirty clothes, you can try almost any other Start behavior tactic: a timer, charting or the 1-2-3 (if the dishes or clothes can be picked up in less than two minutes) can be helpful. Remember to praise compliance from time to time with older kids, and frequently with younger children.

Some parents whose kids are older simply tell them that any clothes that don't make it to the laundry or hamper simply don't get washed. Then the child has to wash them herself. Those are examples of natural consequences. The Docking System can also be considered. You go and get the dirty clothes or dishes from the room, but you charge for your labor. You'll feel better about having to do the job. Make sure you keep your mouth shut about the whole operation and keep the fees reasonable.

Option 2: The Weekly Cleanup Routine

Don't like Option 1? Option 2 is a favorite with many moms and dads. With the Weekly Cleanup Routine, the kids have to clean their rooms only once a week, but according to your specifications. You might explain that the following chores have to be done: pick up, put clothes in hamper, make bed, maybe vacuum. A specific day and time, such as Saturday morning, is chosen, and *the youngster is not allowed to go outside, play or do anything else until his room is done and you've checked him out.* You can check him out by using a chart if you wish.

Cleaning the room is a Start behavior, and you will be rewarding the child immediately after the room cleaning with both freedom as well as praise. If artificial reinforcers are necessary, these rewards will be tallied or recorded at checkout time.

Many parents have tried something like the Weekly Cleanup Routine, but the grownups often ruin the whole procedure by getting into an argument with the child at checkout. Never argue about what needs to be done; make the specifications clear in the first place. For example:

"I'm done with my room. Can I go out now?"
"Your bed's not finished."
"Whadda ya mean? That's good enough."
   (Dad turns to walk away.)
"What's the matter with it?"
"That's 1."
"Oh, for Pete's sake!!" (Goes to finish bed.)

This Dad had already explained before that the bed had to be reasonably neatly made, so there was no need for further talk. His son, though, starts testing, using the badgering tactic, and, after ignoring the badgering once, Dad uses the 1-2-3. If the youngster winds up back in his room with a 3 count and a time-out, that's perfect! He'll have five minutes to make his bed properly.

Tactics for Picking Up Around the House

Let me make one thing perfectly clear: The Close-the-Door-and-Don't-Look method applies only to the kids' rooms. The scheme does not apply to the rest of your house! We won't allow the children to leave your kitchen, family room, dining room, bathrooms and hallways cluttered with their things (as all parents know, kitchen counters and tables are such convenient dumping grounds). You certainly can't close a door and not look when the entire house is involved. Here are some useful routines.

Kitchen Timer and Docking System

These two Start behavior tactics can be very handy in getting the house picked up—especially when you can't avoid having to straighten up on the spur of the moment. When the job has to be done right away, the timer is helpful for picking up rooms, such as family rooms and kitchens. If a surprise guest is coming over, you may not have much time to play around:

> "Hey, kids. Mr. and Mrs. Johnson are coming over in forty-five minutes. I'll need all your stuff out of the kitchen by then. I'm setting the timer."

When using the timer like this, it's perfectly OK (and fun) to add an artificial reward if the room is done within a certain time. Or even an artificial punishment if it's not; they don't do it, they pay you. Just be sure not to use artificials for everything you ask the kids to do. Your praise should be enough reward most of the time—and don't forget that part of a child's satisfaction when you praise him is knowing that he did something that made you happy.

The Garbage Bag Method

This procedure has been a favorite of parents for many years. The deal is this: You first encourage the children, as much as possible, not to leave their stuff lying around the house. You're not going to expect perfection. "Stuff" includes clothes, DVDs, books, papers, toys, Barbies, shoes, pens, comics, electronic games, videos, fossils and so on.

Next, you tell the kids that at a certain time every day, their things have to be removed from the public areas of the house and returned to their bedrooms. Maybe you pick 8 as the cutoff time. Anything left out after 8 will be picked up by you and put into a big garbage bag or some other container, and the child will lose the right to use those items until 6 p.m. the following day. You can set the times however you want.

Some parents threaten to actually throw away the things they find that are not put away. There are two problems with this notion. First, if you do throw away some of your children's possessions, that's pretty harsh (parents have done it!). After all, they're just kids and don't have an inherent desire to pick up after themselves. Second, it's likely you won't really throw the stuff away, you'll just go blustering around about that possibility and about how unfair your life is. In this case, you are simply making a useless, empty threat, and the kids will catch on to you right away.

> **Quik Tip**
>
> Your kids do not have a right to mess up your entire house! Tell the children that by a certain time every day, anything of theirs that you find lying around will be confiscated and unavailable to them until a certain time the following day. Pick up the kids' things without grumbling or lecturing. You'll soon find that before the magic hour comes each day, the youngsters will be scurrying around to salvage their possessions.

So imagine you're using the garbage bag routine and have picked 8 p.m. as the cutoff time. At 7:50 you remind seven-year-old Caitlin that her things need to be picked up. She doesn't respond because she doesn't really think you'll do anything. At 8:05, however, when you quietly begin walking around with a large plastic bag and have already claimed five of her prize possessions, Caitlin becomes a believer. She runs around frantically grabbing whatever of hers she can find before you get to it and yelling, "This is stupid! This isn't fair!"

You consider counting her screaming, but you don't. You put the bag away in your bedroom closet. The following night at 7:50, when you say "Clean up time!" Caitlin scurries around retrieving her things and then she takes them to her bedroom. You say, "Good job, Caitlin—it looks real nice in here!" You are a model of restraint and a motivational wizard.

The 55-Gallon Drum

This next plan is one that I cannot take credit for. The idea was described to me by a lady I spoke with on the phone many years ago. She told me that picking up around her house had never been a problem. This resourceful mother kept a 55-gallon, metal drum in the garage, which was right next to her kitchen. Whenever she would find anything of her children's that was out of place, she would simply put the items in the metal drum.

This procedure had become so routine with her four boys, that whenever one of the kids couldn't find something of his, he would simply look in the drum. One day, for example, her second oldest came running into the kitchen and exclaimed, "Mom, I can't find my gym shoes. Are they in the drum?" "Yes," was mother's reply, and the incident was over.

You say you don't happen to have a 55-gallon drum handy or your kids couldn't reach in there if you did? A large box will do fine.

Chores

By now you could probably write this section on chores yourself! We only need to make a few points. First of all, praise your little ones (five and under) whenever they help out, but don't expect them to be able to remember or to sustain work projects for more than a few minutes. Second, when the kids are approximately seven and over, consider using the Family Meeting (see Chapter 22) to discuss and divide up the jobs that regularly need to be done. This planning will help you avoid the Curse of the Spontaneous Request, which we mentioned earlier.

Third, charting is an excellent tactic for chores. The chart serves both as a reminder of what needs to be done and a record of how well the task was accomplished. When charting chores, consider trying only natural reinforcers (praise, the chart itself and job satisfaction) initially. See how far you get with naturals and only use artificial rewards (allowance, points, etc.) if you're not getting anywhere because the task is so obnoxious or foreign to your youngster.

Fourth, the Docking System is also perfectly suited to chores. If the kids don't do what they're supposed to, you quietly do it for them and they pay you. The payment should not be accompanied by a parental lecture about responsibility. Also be forewarned that some kids will be happy to simply pay you for doing their jobs, and their chore-completion behavior will not improve. What do you do in this case? You can up the ante— they pay more for you to do the chore. Or you can just take the money and run. Consider this an introduction for your child to the workings of a service economy: You don't get free service, you pay for it. There's a lesson in that for your kids.

One final word about pets. Caring for an animal is obviously a chore. When they are overwhelmed with excitement about getting a cat or dog, most kids don't realize that eventually having this animal will mean having to regularly complete boring tasks, such as feeding, watering, cleaning up and brushing. When it comes to pets, our Start behavior tactics are not all equally helpful. Praise, the use of a timer, and charting can all be useful, of course. The natural consequences tactic is inappropriate, however, because this method endangers the animal. Perhaps the best method for pets is the Docking System, because you can care for the pet while your child is learning to be more responsible.

With regard to pets, however, the best advice for parents is this: Don't get any animal that you don't want to take care of yourself.

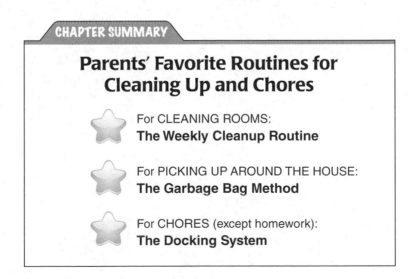

CHAPTER SUMMARY

Parents' Favorite Routines for Cleaning Up and Chores

For CLEANING ROOMS:
The Weekly Cleanup Routine

For PICKING UP AROUND THE HOUSE:
The Garbage Bag Method

For CHORES (except homework):
The Docking System

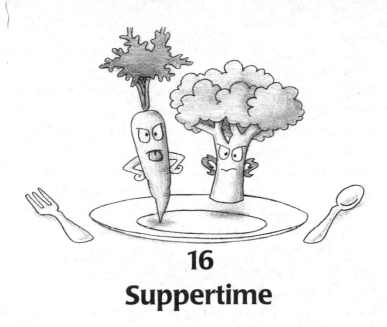

16
Suppertime

It's a fact: Vegetables have always disliked small children.

They say mealtimes are supposed to be a time for family togetherness and family bonding. Dinnertime is a time to open up, talk about your day and enjoy everybody's company. Unfortunately, it too often happens that when you mix together some general childhood fidgetiness, a little sibling rivalry, a finicky vegetable-eater or two, and tired adults, you've got a recipe for an unpleasant occasion.

Picky Pete Who Would Not Eat

Here's a situation most parents have experienced at one time or another. It's suppertime at the Jenkins' house. Peter, however, is not a happy camper. He's picking unenthusiastically at his food:

> Mom: "Come on, Peter. Let's get going."
> Peter: "I'm not hungry."
> Dad: "What did you have to eat after school?"
> Peter: "Not that much."
> Dad: "Then how come you're not eating?"
> Peter: "I am eating!"
> Mom: "No you're not!"

Peter: "We never have anything I like."

Silence. Frustrated parents look at each other and continue eating.

Peter: "Why do I have to eat this stuff?"

Mom: "Because, you know, you want to grow up to be big—strong. You need energy."

Peter: "But I don't like any of it."

Mom: "OK, if you don't finish, there will be no dessert and nothing else to eat before bed. Do you understand?"

Alicia (Peter's sister): "I like what we're having."

Peter: "Oh, shut up!"

Dad: "Peter, you've got five minutes to finish."

Peter: "Dog food's better than this junk!"

Dad: "Up to your room, right now, young man! That's no way to talk to anyone!!"

Peter stomps up to his room. Alicia takes another big bite.

This scene is not a warm and friendly family interaction. This episode has all the elements for disaster: one picky eater, two fighting sibs and two weary parents who are talking too much and asking silly questions.

Here are several routines to help avoid this kind of trouble.

Small Portions and a Kitchen Timer

Quik Tip
Try this with your finicky eaters. Give the kids super-small portions and then set the timer for twenty minutes. If the children finish before the timer goes off, they get their dessert. You may not nag or prompt—the timer will do that for you.

Do you have fussy eaters like Picky Pete? Get out a kitchen timer and set it for twenty minutes when you all sit down at the table. Tell the kids they have to finish their dinner in that time. If they do finish the meal in twenty minutes, they get their dessert. *You're not allowed to prompt anyone to eat; that's what the timer is for.*

When starting the kitchen timer method, initially give your hard-to-please children very small portions of foods they don't like. Even ridiculously small, if necessary, such as three peas, a tablespoon of scalloped potatoes, two bites of pork chop. Research shows that children who are exposed to new foods, but not forced to eat them, will often come around and start to enjoy some of the more exotic possibilities. That result is a lot more healthy in the long run for them.

If the kids goof around or fight at the dinner table, they get counted. If anyone hits a count of three, he is timed out for five minutes while the twenty minutes on the timer keeps on ticking. You may not make comments such as, "Come on now, don't forget the timer's ticking" or "Quit that goofing around and get down to eating, young man!" (How are you going to finish your own meal if you're talking all the time?)

You are probably also aware by now that you would not count the kids for not eating. Eating is a Start behavior, not a Stop behavior. What will help prompt the children to wolf down the chow? The timer: tick, tick, tick. You can, though, praise the kids when they do eat.

What if the timer rings and there is still food on the plates? No dessert—at least yet. The plate goes into the kitchen and onto the counter. Cover the leftovers with plastic wrap. After one half hour has expired, the children have the right to finish the meal if they wish. The food can be quickly nuked in the microwave if necessary. If the youngsters don't ever eat the rest of their meal, that's fine—but still no dessert. Some parents throw the rest of the child's dinner down the disposal when the timer hits twenty minutes, but this procedure seems a little extreme.

Stay on your toes when a hungry little tot who didn't finish her dinner puts the hit on you later for some treats:

"I'm ready for my ice cream now."
"You'll have to finish your dinner first, honey."
"It's all cold."
"We'll just heat it in the microwave for a few seconds and it'll
   be good as new."
"I didn't like it anyway. I just want a little ice cream."
"Now you know the rules, dear, you have to finish what's on
   your plate first. Remember, we didn't give you that much in
   the first place."
"I never get anything!"
"What are you talking about—you never get anything?! That's
   enough of that! Either finish your dinner or stop bugging me!"
"I hate you!"

This interaction was an unfortunate waste of time and *was also very hard on this relationship*. The conversation should have gone like this:

"I'm ready for my ice cream now."

"You'll have to finish your dinner first, honey."

"It's all cold."

"We'll just heat it in the microwave for a few seconds and it'll be good as new."

"I didn't like it anyway. I want just a little ice cream."

"That's 1."

"Then I'll go to bed starving!" (Walks away)

Mom did much better. There were no useless, little-adult explanations, and Mother then ignored her daughter's martyrdom.

The 3-Out-Of-4 Rule

Let's return to the case of Picky Pete. Imagine that Peter's parents sit down, review the mealtime situation, and come up with a new plan. Mom and Dad explain the new deal to their son: If Peter eats three out of four items on his plate, the boy can have his dessert. The serving sizes will be smaller and Peter has to at least taste the one thing he doesn't choose to eat.

The first meal under the new regime goes well. Even though they are a bit nervous, both parents avoid any anxious prompting. Peter finishes his smaller portions of pork, mashed potatoes and peas. After tasting it, he forgoes the salad. He gets ice cream for dessert.

After the mealtime overhaul, the first week passes without any unpleasant incidents. Peter and his parents actually enjoy one another's company; the dinner table conversation is spirited and friendly.

"Pete, how was that movie you saw with your friend?"

"Oh, cool! You guys gotta see it!"

"You really think we'd like it at our advanced ages?"

"Oh, yeah! Let's go—I'll go see it again."

"Well, if your mother's willing, it might be possible."

"Mom, you gotta go. It's so neat! There's this one part where..."

That's the way meals should be. What if Peter and Alicia start fighting? They would both be counted. In our original scene, it would go something like this:

Peter: "But I don't like any of it."

Mom: "OK, if you don't finish, there will be no dessert and nothing else to eat before bed. Do you understand?"

Alicia (Peter's sister): "I like what we're having."

Peter: "Oh, shut up!"

Mom: "That's 1 for each of you."

Some of you may wonder why Alicia should be counted. All she did was say, "I like what we're having." Can you guess the answer? It was all in her rose-colored-but-competitive timing.

The Divide-And-Conquer Routine

Many parents seem to feel that there is a federal law dictating that every family eat supper together each and every night of the year. This is the time, the experts claim, for "family togetherness" and for each person to "share his or her day" with everyone else. Sometimes, however, it seems that dinner becomes a time for people to share their *hostility* toward everyone else. Tempers as well as appetites can be lost.

What can a parent do to improve this situation? One solution, obviously, is not to eat together every night. Though some people consider this sacrilegious, it sure beats fighting all the time. Now you only have to fight every other night!

Seriously, sometimes you might consider feeding the kids first or letting them eat in front of the TV for once. Or, now and then, let the kids eat wherever they want to, as long as they bring back their dishes. Then Mom and Dad can eat in the kitchen or have a peaceful dinner together later, or if you're a single parent, you might want a little time to yourself once in a while.

Key Concept

Who says you have to eat dinner together every single night of the year? Consider having some special nights where each person eats wherever she wishes. Or—better yet—have some nights where one parent takes one child out to eat. It's different and it's fun!

Another idea is for each parent to periodically take one child out to dinner as a kind of special occasion. Once a week isn't a bad idea at all. This one-parent, one-child setup is one that the kids love. It's also one where sibling rivalry is not possible, so the parent is much more relaxed and able to enjoy himself.

Think about suppertime. Eating supper should be a pleasant experience. In fact, with most children, eating is a natural and enjoyable activity that doesn't require much parental intervention. With a little planning you can enjoy your evenings a lot more.

CHAPTER SUMMARY

Possible Suppertime Routines

- Small portions and a kitchen timer
- The 3-Out-Of-4 Rule
- The Divide-And-Conquer Routine

17

Homework

A sickening stack of seemingly unsolvable subjects

Homework civil wars make school nights miserable for the whole family. Schoolwork battles can go on for two, three or four hours a night. People begin to dread the evening, relationships are strained severely, and the child in question learns to hate schoolwork more and more. There's brother sitting at the kitchen table after dinner staring out the window with a sour look on his face. The boy's favorite sister, who completed her homework years ago, sits in the other room, smugly watching TV. Mom and Dad check into the kitchen every five or ten minutes to badger the distinguished academic. Overall, a rotten end to the day.

How can you make homework time tolerable and efficient?

Spontaneous Requests Strictly Forbidden!

First of all, the worst mistake you can make is to ask your child—just when you happen to think about it—if he has homework. This is an example of a spontaneous request, and your question is sure to provoke hostility. Homework should be a daily *routine*—done at the same time and in the same place as much as possible.

One of the best ways of setting things up is to have the child come home, get a snack, goof around for about thirty to forty-five minutes and then sit down in a quiet spot and try to finish his schoolwork before dinner. Then the whole evening is free. The evening will also then be free of homework hassles for you! For many, but not all, children, afternoon is preferable to evening for homework because the child has more energy.

Don't let your young student do academic work with the TV on. The television is always out to get your attention. Believe it or not, however, music from a CD or iPod may be fine. For many children and teens, music provides consistent background noise that blocks out other household distractions.

Natural Consequences

If you are having trouble with homework for the first time—say with a fourth grader—consider trying the natural consequences approach first. That means you do nothing: Keep quiet and see if the child and the teacher can work things out. So many parents get anxious way too soon about their children's schoolwork, with the result that the grownup prematurely takes charge of the job and doesn't give the youngster a chance to learn—and exercise—true responsibility.

Let your daughter, for example, explain to *her* teacher why *her* work was not completed. And when your daughter later complains to you about how irritated her teacher was with her for not turning her homework in, instead of saying, "I told you so," say, "That must have been embarrassing for you, but I'm sure you'll do better." If this approach doesn't seem to be working after a few weeks, then switch to some of the other alternatives described below.

Natural consequences is obviously not the method to use, however, if you have been having homework problems for years and years. With chronic problems, you will need to take a closer look at why your child is having such a hard time. Children with learning disabilities and attention-deficit problems, for instance, not only need a well-thought-out daily homework routine, these kids may also benefit from tutoring, treatment or other academic accommodations.

Assignment Sheets

Assignment sheets or assignment notebooks can be extremely helpful for kids who have homework troubles. Assignment notebooks tell you exactly what work is due for each subject, which—among other benefits—helps prevent lying about homework. Many schools now have Internet-based "Homework Hotlines," where forgetful-but-fortunate kids can log on after hours to find out what their assignments are.

Part of the idea of the assignment sheet, of course, is that after the child does the work, the parents can check her productions against the list of items to be done. If this is the procedure you are considering, you should routinely include our next two homework procedures: the PNP Method and the Rough Checkout. Failure to do so will result in unnecessary conflict and misery.

The PNP Method

Suppose your daughter has just completed her midweek spelling pretest. There are ten words on the list, and she spelled nine correctly and misspelled one. When she brings you her paper, your first job, naturally, is to point out to her the word she spelled wrong. Right?

Wrong! PNP stands for "Positive-Negative-Positive." *Whenever a youngster brings any piece of schoolwork to you, the first thing out of your mouth must be something positive*—some compliment. You might, for instance, praise the child for remembering to show you her work. After saying something nice about the child's effort, you may then make a negative comment, if it's absolutely necessary. Finally, you conclude your insightful remarks with something positive again. So the procedure is Positive-Negative (if necessary)-Positive.

The Rough Checkout

Our next idea, the Rough Checkout, will also help to make your evenings a lot more pleasant. The Rough Checkout notion is based on the fact that 8 in the evening is no time for scholastic perfection. You have worked all day, and your child has also put in just about the equivalent of a day on a full-time job—before she even started her homework!

Unless there is some major indication to the contrary, if your daughter's schoolwork is anywhere near 80 percent neat, correct and thorough, consider calling it a day and consider the job done. Let your youngster and teacher continue worrying about the assignment tomorrow.

This advice is doubly true for ADHD or LD children who are already having a tough enough time with school. You can also adjust your Rough Checkout criteria to your child's overall achievement level. If, for example, your child is generally an excellent student (A-B average), you might consider raising the required neat, correct and thorough percentage to 90 or more.

Quik Tip

The first thing out of your mouth when your child shows you her homework must be something positive—even if it's just that she brought her work to you. And remember: 8:00 p.m. is no time for academic perfection!

I learned this advice the hard way. A mother once came into my office reporting that her twelve-year-old son was getting more depressed, more irritable and more distant from everyone in the family. It turned out that homework was a major problem for this boy every night. The lad would finish his assignments and bring them to his father for checkout. That was the good news. The bad news was that if the work was not absolutely perfect, Dad would tear it all up and make his son start over!

So, if your youngster's work is for the most part neat, correct and complete—but not perfect—consider the PNP procedure. Don't tell the child, of course, that his schoolwork is superb, because it's not. Just say that the work is good and praise some specific parts of what he has done. Perfectionist parents who squirm at this suggestion need to stay in touch with the emotional realities of childhood.

Charting for Homework

A daily charting system can be a godsend when it comes to improving academic work and decreasing homework hostilities. This is especially true when charting is combined with the Rough Checkout and Positive-Negative-Positive methods and when spur-of-the-moment homework requests are avoided. Here's an easy arrangement that can be used.

Since it's usually the older kids who have trouble with homework, a five-point scale instead of stickers can be used on the chart. Five is the highest mark and one is the lowest mark. A child can earn one point for each of the following things:

- Neat: 1 point
- Correct: 1 point
- Thorough: 1 point
- No complaining: 1 point
- Starting on your own at the right time without being reminded: 1 point

Total possible score: 5 points

The kids can get each of the first three points by doing better than whatever approximate percentage of neatness, correctness and completeness you have required according to your Rough Checkout rules. The no-complaining point is earned if the youngster doesn't whine or grouse about having to do his schoolwork.

The last point is the crucial one. We sometimes call the fifth point the "Magic Point," because if you can get a child to start his work on his own, in a timely fashion and without being reminded, the battle is more than half won! You can also set up friendly incentive games with this last Magic Point. For example, three days in a row of starting on your own at the proper time earns a bonus point. Or starting more than fifteen minutes early and finishing in a reasonable amount of time earns two bonus points.

Quik Tip

When charting homework performance using 5-point system, the fifth point is the Magic Point. A child earns the fifth point for starting his schoolwork at the right time without being reminded. That's half the battle!

Remember that for many kids with academic handicaps, you may very well have to use artificial reinforcers to help motivate the child over the homework hurdle. Your successful young scholar, for example, might earn a special outing with you, a special meal, part of his allowance or time on a new game for posting a certain number of points during the week. Different rewards may require different numbers of points. Check back to our list of possible rewards in Chapter 13.

Also, don't forget that kitchen timer when dealing with homework.

For instance, the device can be used to help break up the work into smaller, manageable fifteen-to-twenty-minute pieces. A timer also helps keep kids on task. If your child complains that the timer's ticking bothers him, use some kind of sand hourglass, computer or LCD device.

Getting homework time down to some kind of manageable routine can do wonders for your kids as well as for you. Homework won't necessarily become fun, but it should not be a daily agony. If you have tried the tactics suggested here for four to six weeks and you still feel that things are not going well enough, it may be time for a professional evaluation or an evaluation by the school. Vision and hearing difficulties, specific learning disabilities, attention deficits and a host of other problems can make schoolwork way too hard for some kids. A diagnostic workup is especially indicated when a child has academic trouble *both at home and at school.*

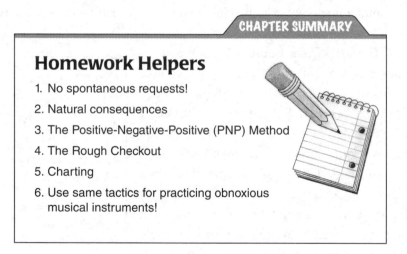

CHAPTER SUMMARY

Homework Helpers

1. No spontaneous requests!

2. Natural consequences

3. The Positive-Negative-Positive (PNP) Method

4. The Rough Checkout

5. Charting

6. Use same tactics for practicing obnoxious musical instruments!

18

Going to Bed—And Staying There!

Lights out?

For many families, putting the kids to bed is a daily nightmare. Although bedtime may technically be 9, at 10:30 the children are still wandering around the house, asking for drinks, telling you they heard a noise outside, or going to the bathroom for the twentieth time. This "routine" may be accompanied by a good deal of arguing, which only ensures that everyone will stay awake to watch the late movie together.

With a little thought, this bad end to your evenings can be eliminated. Your work days are long enough as it is. Many of our Start behavior tactics can be used for bedtime. Put these strategies together and you have some real and wonderfully helpful routines for managing going to bed, staying in bed and nighttime waking. No parental wishful thinking allowed!

The Basic Bedtime Method

Before you do anything else, you set a bedtime for the kids and *stick to it*. The bedtime may vary, of course, depending on whether it's a school night or a weekend, school year or summertime. But exceptions to the rule should be rare. Otherwise, every night, bedtime is open to negotiation, then to testing and manipulation, and then to no one feeling like sleeping.

Let's say you have a nine-year-old daughter, and you decide that 9 will be the time for her to go to bed on a school night. The Basic Bedtime method goes like this. At 8:30 you set a timer for 30 minutes and tell the child that it's time to get ready for bed. This means that the youngster must do everything (potty, teeth, pajamas, etc.) required to prepare for bed—on her own—and then report to you. Make the preparation routine perfectly clear. If your child is only two or three or four, you'll have to help her get ready, but the same rewards and consequences will apply.

When the child has completed all the necessary tasks, she reports to you. If she accomplished everything she had to, praise the child for her efforts. Now comes the reward. Whatever time is left between 8:30 and 9 is time for just the two of you. You might sit on the bed to read a story or simply sit and talk. Kids love this kind of one-on-one time with a parent. Stay in the bedroom and don't do anything super exciting.

> **Quik Tip**
>
> The Basic Bedtime Method will save you lots of aggravation in the evenings. The first requirement is that you pick a bedtime—and stick to it! Bedtime cannot be renegotiated every single night.

This special time serves three purposes. First, it is an immediate reinforcer for the child's independently getting ready for bed. Second, the remaining minutes till 9 are a nice time together. And finally, these moments with you help the kids relax and get in the mood—physically and mentally—for going to sleep.

If you have trouble coming up with an inventory of all that needs to be done for the kids to get ready for bed, just think of all the things the children usually tell you *they haven't done* after they are *in bed*, and you'll have the list right away:

"I'm hungry and I need a drink."
"I'm scared."
"I have to go to the bathroom."
"These pajamas itch."
"There's a burglar in the basement."

Etc., etc., etc. Every item on the list should be addressed as well as possible. And remember that a floor fan often helps kids sleep!

One caution here. Don't lie down on the bed. It just so happens that there is a biological law that says: If you are over twenty-five years of age, and it's past 8 in the evening, and you spend more than three minutes in a horizontal position, you'll be out like a light. And the kids will love it! They'll enjoy the comfort and novelty of having you sleeping next to them, but they will also quickly get dependent on this arrangement and start expecting—or demanding—your presence every night.

And now, the grand finale. When 9 rolls around, tuck the child in, kiss her goodnight and leave the room. You have just had a nice time with your youngster and your parenting job is done for the day.

Right? Perhaps not. At this point some parents say, "How naive you are; when I leave she's right behind me!" or "If I go down to the kitchen, she's sure to show up in less than three minutes." What if your daughter won't stay in bed after 9?

Getting Out of Bed

Some kids just can't seem to stay in bed after you tuck them in. While you try to go about your business, they are always coming up with some new reason for getting out of bed. Why? Usually it's because the children are either 1) scared, 2) bored or 3) both.

When my son was eighteen months old, he climbed out of his crib for the first time. My wife and I were sitting in the living room of our two flat, relaxing and thinking the day was over, when in walked this cute little kid, grinning from ear to ear, proud as punch that he had single-handedly escaped from his crib for the first time in his life. As young parents, we interpreted this event as the end of the known world. We had visions of our little guy getting up at 3 in the morning, calling his friends on the phone, roasting marshmallows on the gas stove or worse.

In desperation—and forgetting temporarily that I was supposed to be a clinical child psychologist—I found some scrap lumber and some bailing twine and built the sides of his crib up about a foot higher all the way around. The contraption worked for two nights.

On the third night our boy figured out a way to scale even these new heights and once again escape. So we had to come up with a new plan. Talking to an eighteen-month-old would have been useless. Not only that, by now our son considered getting out of his crib an exciting challenge. So my wife and I decided that our only choice was to train him some way to remain in bed—or at least in his bedroom.

We put a chair in the door to his room, and after all the bedtime prep was done, one of us (we took turns) just sat in the chair, facing into the hallway. We left the side of his crib down, because putting it up was now useless, and we turned on a floor fan for the noise. We said nothing after bedtime. If our son got out of bed, we put him back. After that we'd give up putting him back in bed, and he'd just fall asleep on the floor. Then we'd cover him and leave, because if we tried to pick him up he'd wake up.

> **CAUTION**
>
> Never forget one very important fact: If a child won't stay in bed at bedtime, the longer he is up and the farther away he gets from his bedroom, the more reinforcement he will get from that activity. Your job? Cut him off at the pass.

After a week or two, he started staying in his bed and going to sleep with no fuss. What a relief! He found our presence in the doorway comforting, even though we weren't talking. In another week or so, we no longer had to sit in there. A couple of months later, our little lad graduated to a junior bed.

The strategy for handling kids' getting out of bed is based on a basic psychological principle: *If a child gets out of bed after bedtime, the longer he stays up, the more reinforcement he gets for this behavior.* And the more he will want to keep getting out of bed in the future. The essential conclusion, therefore, is that you have to "cut him off at the pass"—the doorway to the room. This tactic is no fun for Mom or Dad, but bedtime is no time for wishful thinking. Bedtime is also no time for ridiculous conversations with little kids about why they should stay in bed.

If you have a child who is over five or six, you might be able to use charting to encourage the youngster to stay in bed. If you are using charting with bedtime, however, you cannot tell the child right away how he did, because if he does really well, he won't be awake. Therefore, there will be a long delay—till the next morning—before he finds out how you rated him. But charting can still work, so keep it in mind.

Nighttime Waking

Many children go through periods when they wake up at night and present themselves at your bedside with some kind of vague request for assistance. Some kids may get out of bed a dozen or more times per night, while others will just make a little noise and then go back to sleep.

Nighttime problems are among the hardest to handle, because in the middle of the night most parents aren't quite in their right minds—and neither are their kids. It can also be very aggravating to be awakened from a sound sleep, and sleep deprivation itself can have a very bad effect on your next day at work.

When our daughter was seven, she went through a phase in which she would appear at our bedside in the middle of the night. When we would ask what the problem was, she would say something nonsensical, such as "The elephant ran away." Of course, at 2 a.m. you're not thinking clearly either, so we would respond with something equally ridiculous, such as "Well, where did he go?" These strange episodes went on for several months until we worked out the nighttime waking procedure that I'm about to describe.

Below are a number of steps that have proved to be effective in responding to nighttime episodes. When these steps are carried out consistently and calmly, most kids will get back to sleeping through the night in a few weeks. Remember: If ever there was a time for our No-Talking and No-Emotion rules, it's in the middle of the night!

1. *Accept some waking as normal.* Treat periodic nighttime waking as a temporary stage. This way of thinking will help you be less upset. Obviously, if the problem has been going on for the last four years, it's not a temporary stage. Talk to your pediatrician about the problem.

2. *Don't go to the child's room unless you must.* When do you have to go to the child's room during the night? If she is really upset or won't quiet down, you'd better check things out. On the other hand, many kids will make some noise, fuss around for a while and then go back to sleep. Give them a chance to do so.

3. *No talking and no emotion.* These calming rules apply doubly for nighttime, because talking and emotion—especially anger—wake everyone up. Have you ever tried to sleep when you're furious? You can't. In the middle of the night, even asking a child what's wrong is usually pointless, because the child is groggy, not in her right mind and can't tell you much that's useful.

4. *Assume the child has to go to the bathroom.* Your son appears at your bedside at 2:30 a.m., mumbling incoherently. Somebody is probably going to have to get up. This is an interesting situation, one in which certain people—especially the fathers—could win Academy Awards for sleeping performances. Dad's snoring deepens and the covers go over his head. Even though they don't or can't say it, many kids are awakened by the need to go. But they're so groggy they can't verbalize the physical sensation. So try steering or carrying them to the toilet and see what happens. Don't ask the youngster if he has to go.

5. *Be gentle and quiet.* Handle and guide the children softly as you stagger through the dark. Don't push them around, even though you may be irritated. You want the kids to remain sleepy.

6. *No lights!* Lights wake parents and children up very quickly, which then makes it hard to go back to sleep. Your eyes should be dark-adapted in the middle of the night, so stagger around as best you can.

7. *Don't let the child sleep with you regularly.* Sleeping together can become a habit that's hard to break later on. Unfortunately, letting the child crawl in bed with you is the easiest way to quiet him down right at the time. In addition, staying in bed certainly is tempting, but you will pay for these moments of weakness in two ways. First, you will pay right away if the child really has to go to the bathroom, because he will remain squirmy. Second, you will pay later on when you cannot get the lad to return to his room without his having a tantrum.

One exception to this rule is this: If there's a terrible storm going on outside, complete with thunder and lightning, let the kids sleep on the floor next to your bed with sleeping bags and pillows. They'll do it, and they'll appreciate the psychological comfort. We had this deal with our kids when they were little. During any stormy night, within forty-five seconds of the first thunderous bang outside, our bedroom door would open and two small forms would appear. Each had a sleeping bag in one hand and a pillow in the other. It was cute. Without saying a word, the kids would plop down on the floor and immediately go back to sleep, suddenly oblivious to the storm. That's what parents are for.

Dancing in the Dark

Now, using our seven nighttime steps, let's see if we can persuade a few little tykes to go back to bed—and back to sleep.

Josh, age 9. Josh has been sleeping regularly through the night. Tuesday night, however, he watches a rather scary movie on TV. At 2:45 a.m. you hear a few short, anxious and disconnected sentences. Waiting for a few minutes to see if he'll awaken or get up, you don't go to his room. After a few minutes he goes back to sleep and is peaceful for the rest of the night.

Rachel, age 6. Rachel has been restless in bed for a few consecutive nights, but she hasn't gotten up. Thursday night, however, she appears at your bedside, shakes you by the arm and says she's scared.

You say nothing, get up, put your arm gently around her shoulder, and steer her to the bathroom. She sits on the toilet for awhile, with no lights on. Rachel does have to go to the bathroom. When she's finished, you guide your daughter gently back to bed, tuck her in and give her a kiss. You wait for a second by her door, see that she's falling asleep, and after she's quiet for a few minutes, you go back to bed.

Jim, age 4. Jim has been getting up several times a night. He won't go back to bed by himself and starts making a fuss if you tell him to. You can't tell if he's frightened or if it's something else. If you take him to his room, he cries or starts yelling when you try to leave. He says he wants to sleep with you. You know he's not sick—he just had a physical.

This situation is more difficult, obviously, than the first two examples. You don't want Jim to wake everyone in the house, but you don't like the idea of giving in to his testing either. What should you do?

When Jim appears at your bedside, you escort him to the bathroom first—no lights, no talking. He does need to urinate. Then you take him back to his room, put him in bed and tuck him in.

Now you know he'll probably cry if you try to leave, so before he gets a chance to even get upset, you get a chair, park yourself by the bed and wait till he goes back to sleep. If you've done the main things right— such as no lights and no arguing—your son should still be somewhat sleepy. Though this routine is not fun, you soon find that the strategy is working. Jim is going right back to sleep.

With some kids this procedure must be repeated several times a night for several weeks before the child starts sleeping through. So brace yourself. Of all the families I've seen in my practice, the record for the most times getting up in one night is seventeen! This case involved a little three-year-old girl, and we got her to sleep through the night in two months.

If you think you'll have to sit by the bed after tucking your youngster back in during the night, get your chair ready beforehand. Then, after a week or so of using this procedure, gradually start positioning the chair further from the bed.

CHAPTER SUMMARY

Bedtime is NO TIME for wishful thinking.

Start *your* Basic Bedtime Method today!

Part V

Strengthening Your Relationships With Your Children
(Job #3)

19
Sympathetic Listening

Automatic bonding

Now we turn our attention to the final parenting job, strengthening your relationship with your children. Some people call this "bonding." Bond well with your kids and the first two parenting jobs become easier. Do the first two parenting jobs well and bonding occurs naturally. We'll discuss the two most powerful relationship strengthening tactics, sympathetic listening and shared one-on-one fun, in this chapter and the next.

Be a Good Listener

Your children will frequently surprise you with some of the things they'll say, and your first impulse may often be a negative one. Your ten-year-old son, Tom, comes running in the door after school yelling, "My music teacher's an idiot!" What should you do? You may feel like saying, "That's no way to talk!" You could count—after all the boy is screaming.

But think for a second. He is *not* screaming at you, he *is* upset about something and you don't know what it is. Your priority? Find out what happened and give the child some support. His being angry is no crime, and his outburst couldn't be testing and manipulation, because you didn't do anything to frustrate him. Here is a time for some sympathetic listening. The conversation might go something like this:

Tom: "My music teacher's an idiot!"

Mom: "Tell me what happened."

Tom: "She made me sing in front of the whole stupid class, and only one other kid had to do it. She didn't care, but all my friends were laughing at me!"

Mom: "What did she make you sing?"

Tom: "I don't know, some jerk hymn or something."

Mom: "That must have been awfully embarrassing."

Tom: "I'm going to flunk her class—on purpose!"

Mom: "Boy, I haven't seen you this mad for a while! So what happened when you had to sing?"

Tom: "She makes me stand in the front of the room, then she plays her idiot piano, and I don't even know the words! I could see Dave was giggling and trying not to laugh. I'd like to see him do it!"

Mom: "So you thought it wasn't right for her to make you do it when no one else had to."

Tom: "Yeah. Why are they picking on me all the time? What a totally ignorant school." (Tom leaves to get a snack.)

Sympathetic listening is a way of talking to someone with sympathy or empathy (the distinction between the two isn't important here). Listening is very respectful of another person's thoughts and feelings, because the listener doesn't just sit there, but instead attempts to see the world through the other person's eyes.

When you are listening to your child, you are—like the mother above—forgetting your own opinions for a while, suspending judgment, and committing yourself to completely understanding how the child saw a particular situation (you don't have to agree with him). In our example, Mom is not thinking that her son is being disrespectful or that he caused the trouble. Nor is she formulating her own response.

Sympathetic listening, therefore, tries to accomplish two things: 1) to understand what another person is saying and thinking—from his or her point of view, and 2) to communicate back and check that understanding with the person doing the talking. The listener is an active participant in the conversation, not someone who just sits and nods from time to time (although that's not so bad either when you're totally beat!).

Sympathetic listening is not easy for parents. Once you get past the point of feeling artificial or passive, however, you can sometimes pleasantly knock the kids right off their feet. Listening is an excellent way to begin any lengthy, serious conversation and being respectfully listened to is a great self-esteem builder for kids.

> **Quik Tip**
> Sympathetic listening is very respectful of your child's thoughts and feelings. But listening isn't easy—you have to learn to keep your own opinions to yourself for a while!

How Do You Do Sympathetic Listening?

First, you get yourself in the proper frame of mind: "I'm going to hear this kid out—even if it kills me—and find out exactly what *he* thinks." Then several different approaches can be used, and once you get used to them the whole process should feel very natural. Your listening strategies include openers, nonjudgmental questions, reflecting feelings and checks or summaries.

Openers. You can start with what are called "openers"—brief comments or questions designed to elicit further information from your child. These comments often require self-control, and are especially difficult when you are caught off-guard. Openers may also appear incredibly passive to you, but remember that parental listening must precede any problem-solving discussion. If discipline or other action is necessary, worry about that after you've gotten the facts.

Openers can be very simple, such as "Oh?" "Wow!" "Yeah" or "What?" An opener can be anything that communicates that you are ready and willing to listen sympathetically, including nonverbal behavior, such as sitting down next to the youngster or putting down the paper to look at him. In the example above, Mom's opener was "Tell me what happened."

Nonjudgmental questions. After openers, questions are often necessary to further your understanding of what a child is talking about. To be effective, these questions must not be loaded or judgmental. "Why did you do a stupid thing like that?", "What's your problem today?" or "Why are you bugging me now about this?" are not good questions. These comments will inspire argument or silence.

CAUTION

1. You are a **good listener** if, while your child is talking, you are sincerely trying to understand what he is saying.

2. You are a **bad listener** if, while your child is talking, you are preparing your rebuttal.

Here are some better questions that keep the talk going and further understanding: "What do you think made you do that?" or "What was going through your mind at the time?" In our example above, Mom asked, "So what happened when you had to sing?" That was a good question.

Reflecting feelings. A third sympathetic listening strategy is called "reflecting feelings." If you are going to tell someone that you think you understand him, try to let him know that you can imagine how he must have *felt* under the circumstances. Sometimes, when you reflect feelings, older kids will tell you that you sound a bit like a shrink. If that's the case, just say, "Sorry, but I'm just trying to make sure I understand what you're talking about."

In the example above, Mom reflected feelings back at two points: "That must have been awfully embarrassing" and "Boy, I haven't seen you this mad for a while!" Other examples of reflecting feelings might include: "You really sound bummed out about that," "That must have really been fun!" or "You were pretty upset with me."

Reflecting feelings accomplishes several things. First, it lets the child know that what he is feeling is OK (it's what he may *do* about it that can be right or wrong). Second, the reflecting response reinforces self-esteem and independence. And third, reflecting feelings also helps diffuse negative emotions so they are not acted out somewhere else. You can bet that if Tom's mother had first said, "That's no way to talk about your teachers!" his anger would have been redirected at her immediately.

Checks or summaries. The name of this tactic may also sound a bit fancy, but the idea is simple. From time to time during a talk, it is helpful to check out whether or not you are really getting a good idea of what your youngster is saying. Short summaries now and then tell a child that you're really listening and trying to see the world for a moment through his eyes.

Examples of checks or summaries might be: "Sounds like you're saying that our rules for chores favor your sister," "You felt it was your worst day at school this year," or "You wish I weren't gone so much so we could do more together?" In the example above, Mom's summary was this: "So you thought it wasn't very fair for her to make you do it when no one else had to." That was a nice, sympathetic comment.

Good listening is a communication skill, but it is also an attitude. Your attitude, not your child's. It's the attitude of sincerely trying to figure out what someone else is thinking even if you don't agree. This, of course, is a different kind of job if you're talking to a two-year-old or a ten-year-old. You'll also find that if you listen well, you learn a lot about what your children think about life. That's important as you monitor their psychological and emotional growth. Start listening now, because you'll certainly want to stay in touch with your kids when they're teens!

> **Quik Tip**
> Listening is a skill, but it's also an attitude— on your part. You'll learn a lot about what your kids think about life. Better start listening now, because you're definitely going to want to know what your kids are thinking when they're teenagers!

Sympathetic Listening and Counting

So listening helps you to understand your children and listening also helps to diffuse negative emotions. That's fine, but if you listened *all the time*, you wouldn't be any kind of a disciplinarian. Sympathetic listening, by itself, has nothing to do with setting limits and enforcing rules. Imagine this scene:

Son: "Mom—you idiot! My best T-shirt's still in the wash!"

Mother: "You're feeling pretty frustrated with me."

This parent's response is overly nice. It is also inappropriate. The child's disrespect is way out of proportion to the situation and should be confronted, probably by counting.

On the other hand, if you counted *all the time* whenever the kids were upset, you wouldn't be a very understanding parent. Your kids would correctly perceive you as only an instrument of discipline—or worse.

Imagine this summertime scenario:

"I'm bored."

"That's 1."

That's a pretty insensitive and unnecessary response. Your kids certainly won't want to talk to you very often! So how in the world is a parent supposed to know when to listen and when to count? Sometimes this decision is easy, but often it's not. Our general guideline is this: Discuss problems, count attacks.

Discuss problems. When a child is upset about something, but not being disrespectful to you, it's time to listen and discuss the problem. "Mom, my best T-shirt's still in the wash" might lead to a practical discussion about what to do about the clothing shortage.

Or try this. Your eleven-year-old son, in the car on the way to soccer practice, says, "Our family is so boring." You might want to say, "You're not so hot yourself." Wrong. You should listen and be sympathetic. "I've never heard you say that before. What's on your mind?" is better.

Some children's comments may give you pause, but they're not really attacks. If a parent uses a little active listening, the emotion may be diffused:

"Why are you making me do this stupid homework now!?"

"Homework's a real bummer, isn't it?" (Reflecting feeling)

"Oh, brother." (Child starts his homework with a sigh.)

Happy ending for parent; semi-happy ending for kid.

Count attacks. "Mom—you idiot—my best T-shirt's still in the wash!" is an attack from the start, and many parents would give an immediate 3 for the "idiot" remark.

Sometimes listening doesn't work as well as you'd like. Keep the 1-2-3 ready in your back pocket. The homework conversation above might have gone like this:

"Why are you making me do this stupid homework now?!"

"Homework's a real bummer, isn't it?" (Reflecting)

"Yeah, I hate it!"

"Boy, you really don't like it, do you?" (Reflecting)

"I could be rollerblading with Jason."

"You'd really prefer to be outside playing." (Summary)

"DON'T JUST SAY BACK EVERYTHING I SAY!"

"That's 1."

Overparenting: The Opposite of Listening

Another good way to strengthen a relationship is to avoid what we call overparenting. Overparenting involves forcing unnecessary comments down a kid's throat, making the child feel aggravated and put down. While sympathetic listening encourages independence, overparenting discourages it. Parent squawks, kid "listens."

A while back, I was in a grocery store standing in front of the dairy case. As I was trying to decide which kind of milk to buy, I noticed a mother with a girl, about nine, pushing a cart and coming around the corner toward me. As they came closer, the mother said loudly and anxiously, "Now watch out for that man over there!"

I'm an average-sized guy; there was no way this girl was not going to see me. Even if she had been traveling at 40 miles per hour, she would still have had plenty of room to stop before breaking my legs. Mom's comment was an example of what we sometimes call "overparenting." Overparenting refers to *unnecessary* corrective, cautionary or disciplinary comments made by parents to kids.

Anxious parent, angry child. Adults who overparent usually do it repeatedly and overparenting has predictable, negative effects on children. The first negative reaction is what we call the "Anxious Parent, Angry Child" syndrome. Continually expressing unnecessary worries about kids *to* the kids irritates the youngsters because it insults them. The parent's basic message is this: "I have to worry about you so much because you're incompetent; there's not much you can do on your own without my supervision and direction." No child likes to be put down, and overparenting is definitely a put-down. Overparenting comments can be unnecessary for several reasons:

1. The child already has the skill necessary to manage the situation. Example: the little girl in my grocery store story.

2. Even if the child doesn't have all the necessary skills to manage the situation, it would be preferable for the youngster to learn by direct experience. When we moved into our first house, the kids were about two and four. I'd watch them playing outside with other children, and every five minutes or so I'd see some kind of dispute that I thought needed my intervention. Then one day my wife asked me how I thought the kids survived all day while I was at work. No eyes poked out, no broken arms, no deaths. That shut me up. I'd been overparenting the whole neighborhood.

3. The issue is trivial. Mike and Jimmy are out in the front yard playing catch with a baseball. Jimmy's Dad is washing the car in the driveway while the neighbor, Mr. Smith, is cutting his grass next door. Mike misses Jimmy's throw and the ball rolls over toward Mr. Smith, who smiles and tosses it back. Dad tells the two boys they will have to go somewhere else or stop playing catch. Should Dad have kept quiet? Yes, he should have. Let the two lads work it out with Mr. Smith, if necessary. The boys were having innocent, constructive fun, and Mr. Smith probably enjoyed trying out his old pitching arm again!

Want to encourage independence in your children? Be a good listener and avoid overparenting.

CHAPTER SUMMARY

Sympathetic Listening Quiz:

1. Melissa bounds through the door after school and yells, "I hate my teacher!"

2. A teary Sally says, "I don't think Abbey wants to be my friend anymore."

3. At bedtime Marty explains, "I don't want to go to school tomorrow — I have to give a speech."

4. Ben catches you off guard with "Going to Aunt Mary's is no fun. Can I stay home?"

What would you say in each of these situations?

20

Real Magic: One-on-One Fun

Play hard with your kids.

Show me any two people who have fun together frequently and I'll show you a good relationship. Shared fun provides a necessary nutrition to a personal relationship. Whether they are young or old, people who have regular fun together like each other—period. For many families these days, however, this much-needed enjoyment gets put on the back burner because of the unfortunate focus on two things: work and whole-family activities.

Work, Work, Work

Do you remember how you got married? Most of us started out by dating another person. By and large, that meant fun. Dating was going to the movies, food, endless getting-to-know-you talks, travel, shopping, parties with friends and a whole host of other activities.

Then we went on to make what was perhaps one of the most illogical decisions of our entire existence. We reasoned as follows: Think of all the fun we're having now, and we're not even married. We're only together *half* of the time. Once we're together *all* the time, our good times will double!

That's what we believed. What was illogical about that thought had to do with the fact that getting married is fundamentally a decision to *work together*. Now we'll plan the wedding, now we'll get jobs, now we'll have a baby, now we'll buy a condo, now we'll decorate the condo. The former fun got subordinated to work. Gradually you realized your relationship was getting more strained, and you looked at your spouse one day and thought: "You're not as much fun as you used to be."

Quik Tip
To like your kids you must enjoy them regularly. And for them to respond well to your discipline, they must enjoy and like you too. That means only one thing: You'd better find regular time to play with your youngsters!

In the long run, of course, marriage is a mixture of work and play. The successful couples are the ones who can find the happy balance. But since work fills our time so naturally and aggressively, finding that balance really boils down to maintaining sufficient time for shared fun. If you asked me what's more important in a long-term relationship, communication or shared fun, I would answer "Fun."

The same is true in your relationship with each of your children. To like the kids you must enjoy them regularly. And for them to respond positively to your discipline, they should enjoy and like you. Yes, there is work to be done, but it is absolutely critical that you find time to play

Unfortunately, in the hustle and bustle of everyday existence, many of the daily encounters between parent and child go something like this:

"Time to get up."
"Here's your breakfast. No TV till you're done."
"Got your book bag?"
"You don't have time to play with the dog."
"Come on now, we're in a hurry!"
"Don't forget your coat."
"Love you, goodbye."

The parent sees the child as a bundle of unpleasant tasks, and the child sees the parent as a bundle of unpleasant directions. *No* relationship will remain healthy when this kind of interaction is the only feeding it gets.

The Odd Focus on Whole-Family Activities

Brace yourself for some bad news: Family fun today is way overrated. We consistently hear, for example, that eating dinner as a family every night is the sure-fire way of preventing crime, drug abuse, academic underachievement, teenage pregnancy and a bunch of other social evils.

But going out with the whole crew is not all it's cracked up to be for three reasons. The first is sibling rivalry. Mom and Dad are at the beach, for instance. Six-year-old son says something smart to his eight-year-old sister, who throws her hotdog at her brother, who laughs as it misses and gets full of sand. Now both kids are screaming at each other and everyone on the beach is looking. This isn't fun.

The second reason fun with the entire family doesn't always work is this: The more people you put together in the same place, the greater the chance for differences of opinion and conflict. At 9:30 a.m. on day two of their family vacation, for example, Mark wants to go to Creature Castle, Cynthia wants to go to the pool, Mom wants to have a leisurely cup of coffee, and Dad wants to jog three miles.

There's one more reason family fun is overrated. The best parent-child bonding occurs in one-on-one parent-child interactions. Children cherish alone time with a mother or father, without the presence of their greatest rivals—their siblings. They open up, they feel free and they kind of blossom. It would be a shame to rarely—or never—experience that with one child.

Play with Your Youngster

It's very important, therefore, to take your kids, one at a time, and regularly do something you both like. It's more peaceful because there's no fighting; in fact, there's no chance of fighting. And coordinating different agendas is no problem because there are only two agendas to coordinate.

The possibilities for shared one-on-one fun are endless. Many parents I've worked with over the years like to take a son or daughter out to dinner on a schoolnight while everyone else stays home and fends for themselves. Going to a movie, going shopping, bike riding or just going out for a drive in the car can also fill the bill. One of the nice things about getting out of the house is that no one can interrupt you. Your kids will also like it if you turn your cell phone or BlackBerry off.

One-on-one fun, though, does not have to entail going out, nor does it have to involve spending money. Shared fun can come in little bits and pieces during the day. Little bits of fun can be shared and enjoyed when you are talking, listening, expressing affection or telling jokes. Most children love being able to stay up twenty minutes later on a school night, every now and then, to do something special with Mom or Dad. That something might be reading, just talking or—heaven forbid!—teaching a naïve and inexperienced parent how to play a video game.

The moral of this chapter? By all means, do things together with the entire family, but make sure those times are as enjoyable as possible. If whole-family activities are usually miserable experiences, fix them! But whatever you do about whole-family fun, make sure your days and weeks include regular one-on-one fun with each of your children.

CHAPTER SUMMARY

1-on-1 TIME

The best parent-child bonding occurs during one-on-one fun times. Why? For the kids, they have you all to themselves! And for you, there's absolutely no chance for sibling rivalry. Now there's a formula for success!

21
When Can You Talk?

Like it or not, kids are multimedia learners.

The message in *1-2-3 Magic* about not talking too much worries some people. How are the kids supposed to learn anything, some folks wonder, if adults can never explain anything to them? When can you talk?

The question is both a good one and at the same time a naive one. It's a good one because it recognizes that part of the parenting job is to help your kids acquire the skills, values and behavior necessary for them to make it in the big bad world. The question is naive because it over-emphasizes parental input, talking and one-shot or single-trial learning. The question doesn't understand, in other words, how kids really learn.

Pass on a Game Plan for a Good Life

Your goal in raising your youngsters—in addition to enjoying them—is to help teach—or coach—them on how to leave home and lead a satisfying and happy life. That's what the three parenting jobs described in Chapter 2 are all about. If you reflect on what leading a good life means, you may come up with several important sets of skills:

Meaningful relationships with others. A good life involves establishing and maintaining satisfying, give-and-take relationships with family, friends, coworkers, neighbors and other people. This involves skills like being able to listen, compromise, express yourself and have fun.

Competence in a major life activity. Success at school is one big priority for our kids, but later they'll have to establish careers of their own.

Practical, daily self-management. Kids will need to move out of your house, keep themselves in good physical condition, manage their money and take care of their possessions, such as car, apartment and clothes.

Character: effort, courage, concern for others and the ability to stick by the rules. Character is like the gas in the engine. It's also the antidote to the bad luck that life throws our way and it's critical to adult success.

You value behavior that shows these skills, both in yourself and in your children. You also realize that ultimately your kids' self-esteem will depend on their ability to get along with others, master some line of work, care for the practical aspects of their lives, and display some gumption in doing all of this. You, therefore, want your words (and behavior) to reinforce these values in your kids' actions. All that means— among other things—is that a parent is a values and behavior coach.

But How Do Kids Really Learn?

Kids learn the difference between good and bad behavior, how to get along with others, and how to master life's necessary skills in different ways and from different sources. Several important ways that kids learn include insight, insight plus practice, and social learning or observation.

Insight. One way children learn is through insight provided by adult explanations. Occasionally, but not usually, one explanation is enough. One day my four-year-old grandson came across a pocket knife. When I saw what he had, I told him he couldn't play with that because it was sharp and could cut his finger. He said "Oh," put the knife carefully down, and that was the end of it.

Little Adult explanation, insight, one-trial learning. How nice, but also how exceptional! The same thing didn't work when it came to getting his sister to not climb on the furniture.

Insight plus practice. More often than not, an insight or explanation has to be supplemented by practice. Repetition of just words is not good enough. Adults forget that children's mastery of behavioral skills depends not only on insight but also on behavioral repetition.

You didn't master the art of driving a car by simply reading about it in a book. You did not become a competent driver because your driving instructor told you where the ignition, steering wheel, gas pedal and brake pedal were. Although those concepts were essential bits of knowledge, you still had to go out and practice, practice, practice. And you had to practice under different conditions. You had to drive in good and bad weather, with a pleasant or angry or worried adult, and at times when you were in a good mood or in a bad mood.

Quik Tip

Don't ever underestimate how much *behavioral rehearsal* is required before kids can master skills such as using a fork, not biting other kids, talking in a normal voice when frustrated, organizing homework, remembering to pick up after themselves, and making and keeping friends.

The same is true of your children. Don't ever underestimate how much behavioral rehearsal is required before kids can master skills such as using a fork, putting on their coats, not biting other kids, talking in a normal voice when frustrated, organizing homework, remembering to pick up after themselves, and making and keeping friends.

Social learning (observation). There is another powerful influence on kids' behavior and skill sets, but this one is a two-edged sword. As we all know, kids are great imitators and they learn a lot by watching the behavior of other people. Psychologists call this type of learning social learning. Kids observe everything. Social learning is probably a more powerful influence on what kids think, feel and do than any Little Adult explanation you'll ever come up with.

Children closely watch the behavior of other people, and they pay particular attention to how that behavior benefits or hurts the people doing it. Before you ever opened your mouth with some profound expression of insight, your kids had already been observing how other people *feel, think and behave*. They had been affected by television, news, stories, music, lyrics, and movies. They had seen teachers, peers, actors, actresses, and parents in action. And kids don't miss much.

So What About Talking?

Now let's revisit the question that started this chapter: When can you talk? If the purpose of talking is simply to have fun, the answer is anytime. No problem—have a good time and enjoy the conversation!

If the purpose of talking is to act as a values/behavior coach, however, the answer is not so simple. Lectures, yelling and nagging are all forms of talking; they can happen quite naturally. But these tactics are more likely to discourage identification with your values and decrease behavioral cooperation. When it comes to talking to your kids about how to lead a good life, you must be realistic and know what you're doing.

Quik Tip

It is very likely that all your ideas about your child's behavior are correct. Parents are not stupid and they do not usually go around saying dumb things to their children. Even though your ideas are good, your child is not open-minded during discipline episodes.

When not to talk or coach. Too many parents wait till they're angry about something, then they try to do their constructive chat. But the time when a rule is being enforced is usually a bad time to talk. Why? Because this brief period of time is not a good learning moment for most kids. You are likely to be irritated with your child. Chances are she is mad at you, too. She may at the same time feel anxious, guilty and defensive about what just happened.

Talking during this time of unpleasant emotional arousal produces two problems. First, talking at this point encourages arguing. There are lots of children who do not relish the idea of humiliating themselves by admitting that you—and all your reasons—are correct, while their behavior was absolutely wrong. To save face, therefore, the youngsters may feel obligated to disagree with you.

Second, it is very likely that all your ideas about your child's behavior are correct. Parents are not stupid and they do not usually go around saying dumb things to their children. Even though your ideas are good, your child is not open minded during discipline episodes. At that moment, she doesn't want to hear what you have to say, and your attempts to explain only aggravate her more. This irritation motivates your daughter to contradict what you are saying—even if only in her mind. So what have you accomplished? You have given your little one an opportunity to throw your good ideas into the trash.

When do you talk or coach? Well, how do kids learn? Insight, insight plus practice and social observation are three major ways.

Insight only. Kids will learn some things by means of a single explanation from you. You explain to them how to turn on the dishwasher or you show them how to get to school. Done. That's the good news. The bad news is that very few items fall into this category! Most of the things kids have to learn are more complex. Yet we adults stubbornly cling to the notion that one explanation should do it for things like sibling rivalry, disrespect, getting up and out in the morning, eating right, chores and sleeping through the night. That delusion of ours is called ... well, by now you know what it's called.

Insight plus practice. A ton of kids' necessary learning about how to behave in life is going to fall into the insight-plus-practice category. It's not going to be one-shot and insight only, as much as our Little-Adult-oriented minds might wish it. When it comes to values and behavior, a parent's job is going to be more like *training* than just explaining. Repeated practice and repeated feedback are required.

How does a coach coach? He first shows or explains just what the desirable or undesirable behavior is. Then comes an opportunity for the trainee to practice. Then comes the coach's feedback, then more practice, and so on. The initial explanation to the trainee is the beginning of the insight part, but that insight has to be translated into action by practicing. The coach gives feedback about the trainee's action, praising the good and correcting the bad. The practice-feedback process is repeated and the behavior improves, often gradually.

What is *1-2-3 Magic*? *1-2-3 Magic* is a kind of coach's what-to-say training manual for parents. On the left below are some of the values and behavior you want your kids to learn. On the right are some of the 1-2-3 strategies you can use to teach or coach them to acquire these skills:

Life Skills	Coaching Techniques
• Social skills	• Counting (Job #1)
• Academic and work competence	• Praise, Timer, Docking System, Charting, etc. (Job #2)
• Daily self-care skills	
• Character (effort, courage, following rules, altruism)	• Listening, Fun, 1-on-1 and Family Meetings (Job #3)

So you can coach values and behavior in lots of ways. Calmly counting sibling rivalry, disrespect and arguing, for example, is a point for the importance of getting along with others. Expressing admiration for the long training of a professional athlete says you think the persistence and effort aspects of character are critical in life, even if you don't turn out to be the best. You can also praise your youngsters' homework efforts and attend their soccer games. Listening sympathetically to your kids' opinions about school, friends and the news can boost their confidence, improve your relationship with them, and help them get along with others. All these strategies involve purposeful talking.

Talking can also involve trying to pass on an insight of yours via direct explanation. When prompted by some event (other than misbehavior!), for example, a *mini-lecture* (less than two minutes) about kindness, hard work, doing something for society, ethical behavior and sportsmanship might be useful. You might also discuss drug use, sex and romance, and the pros and cons of technology.

Quik Tip

Kids also relate well to stories—often better than they do to lectures. Stories with a point are a kind of Aesop's Fables approach to values and behavior. The stories might be from your own past or they might be something you saw or read somewhere.

Kids also relate well to stories—usually better than they do to lectures. Stories with a point are a kind of Aesop's Fables approach to values and behavior. The *stories* might be from your own past or they might be something you saw or read somewhere. Stories about courage, effort, working hard to build a successful career, taking care of one's family, and the struggles involved in maintaining personal relationships can all be meaningful to kids.

So when can you talk? If by talk you mean attempting to verbally transmit insight and values, at least be realistic. Don't try this during discipline, keep it short, realize that insight plus practice is required, and listen carefully to what your kids have to say about your message.

What About Social Learning?

As we mentioned before, kids also learn through observing the behavior of lots of other people. That means your children have coaches other than you. In some ways social learning reinforces the values you want your kids to pick up, but in other ways it may work against you.

Imagine you just watched a fairly ordinary adventure flick with your ten-year-old son. Naturally, you both identified with the hero, who, after many extraordinary and harrowing challenges, eventually won out, saved the world and got the girl. The hero's behavior was a powerful social model for your youngster, and some of the values the movie reinforced were the following:

1. Effort and courage will be rewarded.
2. Concern for others is admirable.
3. There's no problem with unprotected sex.
4. In the end good will win out over evil.
5. Physical violence is often a necessary means to getting what you want.
6. Successful male violence is admired by attractive females.

As a parent, you are a values coach, but you have quite a bit of competition for your kids' souls. In the list above, you may like values #1 and #2, be ambivalent about #4, and dislike #3, #5 and #6. As a matter of fact, movies and television dramas often reinforce effort, courage and altruism more than parents do. On the other hand, most parents question the sexual ethics and attitudes toward violence portrayed in many forms of entertainment.

Yes, you are a coach, but your message gets both reinforcement and competition from the rest of your child's world. Your youngsters aren't just going to blindly accept everything you say. What can you do about their social learning?

Model and Monitor

Model. Your behavior talks all the time, and your modeling influence is more powerful than most of your competitors.' You are a big part of your youngsters' social learning. Your showing up for work on time every day, for example, tells your kids the importance of following the rules and the value of effort. Your sympathetic listening to a friend shows that you value concern for others. Your attending a long, continuing education seminar is a plug for self-improvement. Your kids won't miss these messages, especially if they have a good relationship with you.

Monitor. In addition to being a valuable model, you'll want to monitor the kinds of things your children are learning from their other life "instructors," such as teachers, peers, media and Internet. Your youngsters' external behavior will tell you a lot about how they feel about relationships with other people, about school, about their physical condition and about character.

But how do you tap into their inner thoughts and feelings? Here's one way. First, at a time of relative calm and in a 1-on-1 situation, put on your sympathetic listening shoes and make sure they're tight. Then ask this question: "What do people your age think about _____?" Fill in the blank with hard work, bullying, school, what to do when you grow up, doing things that scare you, following the rules, having a best friend, physical exercise, and so on. Adjust the language for the age, listen like crazy, and see what you get!

CHAPTER SUMMARY

How Do Kids Learn?

22
Solving Problems Together

Family Meeting: aggravating but effective

When your children are small, you should be the boss. Your parenting should be a kind of benevolent dictatorship, where you make most of the decisions, you are the judge and jury, and you are gentle and kind. Your children will not decide each day what they have for dinner, when they go to bed, or whether or not they show up for preschool in the morning.

As your little ones get bigger, however, the setup should gradually change. When your children are seventeen, the household should be almost, but not quite, a democracy. Almost a democracy means that your adolescents have a lot more to say about the rules and policies that affect them. This notion also means that as the years have gone by you have been giving your kids more and more independence. Ideally, teens should be making their own decisions about homework, bedtime, choice of friends, clothes and—to a large extent—diet. *Encouraging children's growing independence* is one of a parent's most important challenges.

How do you go about supporting your kids' independence? First, you avoid overparenting like the plague and second, you involve your kids in problem solving efforts through family meetings and one-on-one parent/child meetings.

There are several reasons these get togethers are a good idea. As the kids get older it makes more sense that they have a bigger voice regarding the issues that affect them. In addition, kids will cooperate better with a decision or policy when they have had a say in the development of that idea. And finally, children need the experience of family negotiation to prepare for their own marriages and families. Unfortunately, far too many married adults learn the hard way—when it is too late—that their personal negotiation skills stink.

A good time to start family or 1-on-1 meetings is when the kids are around first grade. Don't try meetings when the children are three or four years old; that's a good way to go insane inside of twenty-five minutes. The family meeting can take place as often as you wish; once every week or two is ideal. One-on-one conferences should be done less frequently or as needed. You can call special meetings whenever a unique problem comes up and your kids can also request a meeting themselves.

How To Run a Family Meeting

The format of the family meeting is simple. One parent is usually the chairperson and has the responsibility for keeping order and for keeping people on task. Older children can take a try at running the meeting themselves from time to time if you think they can handle the job. The chairperson sees to it that the agenda is followed, that each person gets a chance to speak, and that others listen without interrupting.

What is the agenda? Each person in the family brings to the meeting a problem that he or she wants resolved. Then, with each issue, the chairperson guides the group through the following steps:

1. The first speaker describes the problem she wants resolved.
2. One by one, every other person gives his or her thoughts and feelings about that issue. Others try hard to listen.
3. The floor is opened to proposals for solutions; anyone can speak, but one at a time.
4. A solution to be tried is agreed upon. This final idea may combine aspects of suggestions from different people. If there are disagreements, Mom and Dad have the final say.

5. The solution is entered in the computer and a hard copy is posted on the refrigerator.

6. Next person, next problem; steps 2-5 are repeated.

Most solutions are considered experimental, especially if the plan is complex and differences of opinion are large. If the proposed resolution doesn't work, that idea will be reviewed at the next family meeting. Although proposals should be concrete, specific and practical, don't be afraid to make them flexible and imaginative (see The Case of the Disappearing Soda below)!

Sitting through these family meetings is not easy. If you're hoping these will be warm, fuzzy experiences, they're not. In fact, family meetings can be downright obnoxious at times, so it's a good idea to keep them under an hour. Before our family meetings, our kids would grumble and tell us that all their friends thought my wife and I were weird. But once at the meeting, our two youngsters would certainly put in their two cents!

Quik Tip

Many parents agree that the family meeting is one of the most *aggravating* and one of the most *effective* things you can do with your children. Don't ever expect anyone to want to come!

The Case of the Disappearing Soda. When she was nine, my daughter brought this weighty issue to our biweekly family meeting. She explained we usually bought an eight-pack of soda pop, and there were four people in the family. The problem was that she wasn't getting her two bottles. There was never any left! We all listened to our daughter's description of the problem, then Brother, Mom and Dad all threw in their opinions.

After some jockeying around we found a solution: When the eight-pack of pop entered the house, all eight bottles would be initialed with a felt marker: two for Mom, two for Dad, two for Sister and two for Brother. If you drank your two bottles, you were done until the next eight-pack arrived. If you still wanted more pop, you first had to check the eight-pack to see if there were any full bottles left. If there was a full one, you could purchase it for a certain amount from the person who "owned" it. If the person declined to sell, no testing and manipulation was allowed. This agreement was posted on the refrigerator and it worked like a charm.

How to Do a 1-on-1 Meeting

Imagine you have become concerned about the way that your eight-year-old son has been treating his friends when they come over to play. Two things bother you: 1) He makes fun of the other boys and 2) he will only play what he wants to play and will not listen to any suggestions.

What do you do? You make an appointment with your son and you calmly and briefly tell him what you are worried about. Like this: "I'm concerned about how you've been playing with Mark and Kyle. Let's get together some time and talk." Then you get together, just the two of you, and follow the family meeting format described two pages back.

1. You describe the problem. Be brief—no nagging or lecturing. "I'm concerned about your making fun of your friends and not letting them do what they want to do when they're at our house."

2. Ask your son for his opinion of the situation: "What do you think about this?" Do your best sympathetic listening.

3. Next, generate some solutions: "What can we do about this and how can I help out?" Wait for your youngster to come up with ideas first. If he can't or refuses, then come up with your own.

4. Agree on something to try and be very specific.

You don't need to enter the solution in the computer unless your son wants to. Try out the ideas, praise cooperation and tune up the agreement in future meetings. Helpful hints: Before the meeting make sure you're in a good mood, during the meeting make sure your listening shoes are on, and after the summit try a little shared 1-on-1 fun. Good luck!

CHAPTER SUMMARY

Family meetings and 1-on-1 meetings are not always fun. But they help prepare your kids for one of life's ultimate challenges... **Living with someone else!**

23
Kids, Tweens and Tech

As if parenting weren't hard enough already!

Kids' daily consumption of mass communication by means of various tech devices gets larger and larger every year (so does their parents'). Recent estimates tell us that over 7.5 hours per day are spent by 8-18 year olds with TV, cell phones, music, computer, video games, print and movies. Some people claim the real figure should be 10.5 hours, because about three of the daily techcom hours are spent "multitasking," which means doing two or more things (TV, texting, surfing) at the same time.

The Triple Alliance

The power of "techcom" is here to stay. The clout of the omnipresent new screens in our lives is based on a sort of accidental alliance among three groups: our kids, techcom providers and parents. In this alliance kids and techcom providers are active seekers, while parents are often passive participants. What does each group get out of the deal?

Kids. Children get reliable, immediate, fascinating, *non-stop entertainment*. Kids are naturally curious. What better vehicle for satisfying curiosity than the Web? TV, music and video games also provide guaranteed fun—and there's no waiting! The experience is not like living on a farm in the middle of nowhere in the 1850s; it's more like bringing every aspect of the big city—the good and the bad—right into your own bedroom. To kids, tech is brain candy. Kids actively seek new and exciting material, and they have a network of consultants to help them.

Providers. The people who provide this intense experience to kids are not individuals. They are companies. Out of the three-way conspiracy, they get *profits*. There's nothing wrong with making money, and these huge organizations pay their taxes, try to satisfy their shareholders, and provide jobs for hundreds of thousands of people. But a financial bottom line is just that: dollars. These companies are not primarily concerned with what may or may not be in the long-term interests of your kids. Like the children, techcom providers are active and busy seeking new products and clients, and they also have multiple consultants available.

Parents. Now you might wonder how parents could possibly conspire to foment the tech uprising. What do we get out of the deal? Simple: *effective babysitting*. Seven to ten hours per day. Add that to the end of a school day and you hardly have to do anything! We want to see our kids happy. When they are watching TV, phoning friends or furiously working their Xbox 360 consoles, they are happy. They don't fight as much. You are free to recover from your own long work day. *This is not an insignificant benefit*. So parents tend to passively let children and techcom providers hook up. Parents do not use consultants because they do not have time, do not see the need, or feel intimidated by technology.

The triple alliance and media/technology consequences are not run by anybody. The President doesn't run it, the courts don't control it, consumer groups and churches don't have much say. The techcom revolution is like a huge monster charging ahead full speed. Representing both good and bad, the monster is lost—but it's making good time.

Good Aspects of TechCom

The tech revolution is truly remarkable and it has brought a number of positive developments for society and your children. The Internet provides more information than has ever been available before at any one time. Surfing the Web can uncover—in a matter of seconds—facts and images that would have been inaccessible and unimaginable only a few years ago. Kids can research and write term papers using Google—forget walking to the library! In addition, as your children search for this information or play games, they are developing computer skills and, some claim, brain power.

Social networking sites, multi-gadget phones and multi-player video games allow your children new ways to build and foster relationships. Facebook, for example, boasts 400 million users. And although Facebook "requires" a minimum age of thirteen, lots of ten-to-twelve-year-olds sign up simply by swearing that they are thirteen or older.

Cell phone use is also on the rise among older children and teens. About one-third of teenagers send more than 100 messages per day from their cell phones; one-quarter of their text messages are sent during class. Eighty-three percent of these kids take pictures with their phones, 60 percent play music, 46 percent play games and 32 percent exchange videos. All of these activities can be positive experiences.

Positive techcom implications for your relationships with your kids? New ways to connect. Through social network sites or through texting, you can talk with your child in her new languages and formats. Families can watch movies together, dads and moms can learn to play video games with their children.

Bad Aspects of the Tech Revolution

On the flip side, however, there are a number of troubling aspects. Violence is portrayed online, on TV, in the movies, and especially in video games. A typical news broadcast consists of 30 percent ads and 53 percent crime, disaster and war. By eighth grade, kids will have seen about 8,000 murders on TV; they will have committed quite a few murders themselves while gaming. Two-thirds of American homes own a video game console. Popular games include Dead Rising, where you fight waves of zombies, and Grand Theft Auto, where you fight to move up in the underworld.

Perhaps even more troubling is the pornography that is available through new technology. The average age of a child's first exposure to pornography is 11. According to Family Safe Media, the largest group of viewers of Internet porn is children between ages 12 and 17. Another danger is sexual predators. One in seven children who use the Internet regularly report receiving sexually suggestive remarks from someone they don't know, either online or through text messaging.

Sometimes online relationships are hurtful to children through what is called cyberbullying: using technology to victimize others. Many children, unfortunately, love to make fun of other kids. Since the abuse is not face-to-face, it is easier for children to take part in.

Negative influences of techcom on parent/child relations? Arguments can break out about time spent on video games, about cell phone usage and cost, or about the relevance of movie or game ratings. Making matters worse is the fact that in these battles, confident tweens often know more about tech subjects than their nervous parents.

In addition, kids often appreciate something that their parents don't: Today's tech devices change rapidly and their functions overlap considerably. Technology that once was just on the computer is now on the cell phone. What was once on a video game console is now on a hand-held device, the computer and the cell phone. Most devices have multiple uses. Techcom providers are active seekers!

TechPlay and Time

All this technology is a new kind of play for our children, and "techplay" also has a good and a bad side to it. On the bright side, the ability to play and to relax with no particular purpose is one of the healthiest habits you can learn. Techplay can be a pleasant and beneficial way of wasting time. Many super-driven Type A adults don't have this skill, and they pay for this deficiency with their mental, physical and social health.

So what's the problem with techplay? Two things: lack of physical exercise and wasted time. Seven to ten hours per day per kid is a lot. It would be very, very beneficial for their future welfare if kids got into a habit of physical exercise at least one hour per day, especially as they get older. Exercise helps you and your body deal with lots of stressors.

In addition, our kids are still preparing for their futures. That includes their careers. Many people are familiar with Malcolm Gladwell's bestselling book, *The Outliers*. In the book Gladwell describes his "10,000-Hour Rule." He says the key to success in any field is a matter of practicing a specific skill for a total of 10,000 hours. How much is 10,000 hours? Think of this: If you work a full-time job for a whole year, that's 2,000 hours. So 10,000 hours is like five years working full time.

You want to be an excellent piano player? Practice for 10,000 hours. A great basketball player? Practice 10,000 hours. Start your own business? Run long distances? Same thing. If your kids do video games, TV and Internet for eight hours per day for fifteen years of their growing-up time in your home, they will have logged over 40,000 techplay hours.

Did they need that much relaxation? According to *The Outliers*, your children could have become experts in four different areas over that same period. That's absurd, but the point is this: Exorbitant use of tech play can severely restrict your kid's acquisition of key skills—social skills, career talents, physical conditioning and character. So it makes sense that some kind of limits should be placed on this type of recreation so kids can practice and enjoy more useful activities. That's that demanding parenting role again: "My child, I expect something from you!"

What's a Parent To Do?

All this news about technology may make the Amish solution look tempting. Technology, in fact, *is no longer controllable*. But our discussion is not meant to scare you away from all the new techcom gadgetry. Compare your child's use of technology to driving a car. Driving a car is serious business. No competent parent would allow their child to drive without some instruction and agreement for the vehicle's use.

It may seem overwhelming, but let's look at some fairly simple guidelines for making technology a positive part of your family's life. First of all, you're going to *have to talk with the kids* and develop some guidelines for techcom use. In doing this you'll need some of the skills and attitudes we just discussed in Chapters 19 (Sympathetic Listening), 21 (When Can you Talk?) and 22 (Solving Problems Together.).

Second, you're going to have to *know what to talk about*. Below you'll find a list of some of the most important issues you'll want to cover. As you carry on these 1-on-1 or family meetings, keep this in mind:

1. *With tweens (9-12)*, bring up the issue, then listen FIRST to what they have to say. With some tech issues, the kids will have more to teach you than vice versa, so be HUMBLE and listen! Discuss, ask questions, then formulate your agreements. Signed contracts are a good idea.

2. *With kids up to age 8 or so*, you may know more than they do. So you can teach first, discuss, then make your agreements.

Below are the issues you'll want to clarify.

Techcom Selection and Setup

1. Before purchase, the capabilities of each device will be understood.

2. Computers will be kept in public places: not in the bedroom.

3. Consider installing *monitoring* software; monitoring software keeps a record of what your child does on the computer.

4. Install *filtering* software for Internet use; though they are not perfect, filters help block inappropriate sites.

5. Deactivate the online component of techcom gadgets with Internet capabilities that can't be filtered.

6. Set all privacy settings, especially on social networks, to their highest level.

TechCom Input to Your Home

1. Teach your children not to open unexpected emails or spam links, which may lead to porn sites or computer viruses.

2. Check ratings for video games, TV shows, and movies.

3. Include your specific time constraints for techcom use. For example, "Two hours techplay after homework is done."

4. Clarify exactly what websites, movies or games are off limits.

5. Don't leave your own Internet-accessible devices lying around.

TechCom Outputs from Your Kids

1. Discuss not giving out personal information online, such as last name, address, school names, pictures, etc.

2. Discuss not giving out passwords to anyone or changing computer settings without your permission.

3. Discuss meeting online friends in person; agree to accompany them to any first meeting.

4. Establish rules for gossip or cyberbullying.

5. Tell your children what to do if a pornographic image comes up; for example, turn off screen and find a parent.

6. Discuss file sharing with the kids. Some file sharing is illegal, and some filesharing programs can "share" other private files from your computer that you don't want shared.

TechCom Outside the House

1. The guidelines above also apply to locations outside your home.

2. Talk about and roleplay how to manage peer pressure.

While implementing your agreements, expect some testing and manipulation. Expect a lot of testing if you have an eleven-year-old son who is used to gaming six hours per day. On the other hand, praise cooperation and don't model ridiculous tech involvement yourself. If violations of your family agreement occur, consider 1-on-1 meetings first and then use the Major/ Minor System for repeat offenses.

Quik Tip

Most Internet filters and cell phone companies have parental controls that allow you to turn off the device during specified times. This can be very helpful to keep kids off the Internet at night and off the phone during school hours.

In your family and in 1-on-1 meetings you'll also want to make specific agreements about more positive, non-techplay activities, like reading, exercise, work, constructive tech learning, time with friends and time with you. Don't hesitate to occasionally use techplay as a reinforcer for self-improvement activities. Restricting techplay is also a good time-out alternative for Stop behavior. One enterprising parent said the only reason he gave his son a cell phone was so he could take it away (wonder if the cell phone had Internet access?)!

Your Ace in the Hole

In *1-2-3 Magic* our goal is to keep things simple and doable. Unfortunately, to many parents this chapter may appear more complex and intimidating. Hold the phone! There is a workable solution.

You recall earlier we mentioned that in the triple alliance both your kids and the techcom providers were active seekers, and they both made use of consultants. You know who companies use, but you may have wondered whom your kids use for advice. Simple: *other kids and the Internet*. You want the scoop on the latest Super Mario Brothers, call a friend. You want to know how to get around parental controls, same thing, or Google "bypass parental controls."

Believe it or not, without too much trouble you can give up your passive participation in the triple alliance and become an active seeker too. You can access free and helpful experts. They're called *other parents*. All you have to do is make a few phone calls. School counselors or pediatricians may also help hook you up with someone.

Here's what you'll find. About half of the parents you talk to won't be any help because they won't know any more than you do. Twenty-five percent will be somewhat useful, and the final 25 percent or so will be very useful! What question do you ask them? This one: "How do you handle all this new tech stuff with your kids and what do you do about parental controls?" After reading this chapter, using another sympathetic and friendly human being as a guide is the most efficient—and easiest!—way to attack the issue of kids, tweens and tech.

CHAPTER SUMMARY

Fact or Fiction?

Imagine: Lonnie is currently an unemployed cab driver in Baltimore. As a kid growing up in Buffalo, he logged a total of 52,458 techplay hours, mostly TV and video games. He's superb at Grand Theft Auto.

Sarah is running her own company in Seattle. As a child she logged 11,320 techplay hours. She spent the rest of her non-school time in the Girl Scouts, doing volunteer work, sports, babysitting, learning Spanish and working six different jobs as a teenager.

Part VI
Enjoying Your New Family Life

24

Staying on the Wagon

Nobody's perfect.

At this point you are well into your three parenting jobs. You are controlling obnoxious behavior with counting; you are using the seven Start behavior tactics to establish positive routines, and you are consistently working on reinforcing your relationships with each of your children. *1-2-3 Magic* is known for producing results. It works—and it often works in a very short period of time. No magic. Just the logical, consistent application of certain basic principles of parenting technology to the *nth* degree. Like any good thing in life, though, the 1-2-3 takes some work and some thought to keep it going well.

Falling Off the Wagon

Parents are human beings who have good days and bad days. Many people have used the 1-2-3 religiously for years and years. For other caretakers it is a struggle to stay consistent and to remember what they're supposed to be doing.

The problem we're talking about here is called "slipping," or falling off the wagon. It means you start out well with *1-2-3 Magic*, get the kids shaped up, but then slip back into your old unproductive ways of operating. The *1-2-3 Magic* switch sort of goes to the "Off" position. The former status quo has a nasty way of sneaking back up on us. Falling off the wagon can occur suddenly on an especially bad day, or slipping can happen more gradually over a period of months or even years.

> **Quik Tip**
> When you're doing nine things at once, who can remember the No-Talking and No-Emotion Rules? You can!

In the course of a day there's always so much going on. You have to go to work, drive the kids all over the place, feed everybody, answer junk phone calls, help with homework, call your mother, and try to find a little time to read the paper. When you're doing nine things at once, who can remember the No-Talking and No-Emotion Rules?

You can! It's not always easy, but it beats arguing and screaming, which only add to your troubles and make you feel angry and guilty. Remember: *1-2-3 Magic* was specifically created for busy parents like yourself who are inevitably going to get upset from time to time.

Over the long term, slipping can occur for a number of reasons. The most frequent culprits are visitors, illness, travel, new babies and just plain time. Gradually you find yourself talking too much, forgetting your Start behavior routines, and not enjoying your kids anymore. Then one night, you wake up at 3 a.m. and wonder, "What happened to the 1-2-3?"

Emotional Obstacles

Slipping can also occur in certain situations where your thoughts and emotions conspire to throw you off track. In these situations, it's not so much that you forget what you should do. Instead, emotional forces inside, caused by a little bit of screwy thinking, push you toward a bad discipline response.

How do you manage these unwanted tests of your will? Straight thinking—along with a little effort and courage—are often needed. Let's look at a few examples.

Anxiety: What will people think?

Wrong way: You have two other couples over for dinner and you're sitting at the table with them and your son and daughter, ages 6 and 8. The kids start poking one another. Daughter pushes son and says, "Leave me alone!"

One of your guests laughs and says nervously, "Well, kids are always kids, aren't they?" *You think.* "I don't want to embarrass myself and everyone else by disciplining at the dinner table." *You laugh along* with your friend.

Right way (same scenario): You think, "Our friends may wonder what I'm doing, but I'd better nip this fight in the bud." *You say*, "Guys, you're both on a 1." Then you briefly explain counting to your guests.

Anger: Bringing your work home

Wrong way: You've had a terrible day at work, having made two major mistakes and aggravating your boss big time. When you walk in the door, the kids are watching TV and the family room floor is covered with books, papers, pens, toys and just general junk. *You think*, "Why can't these kids ever put anything away!?" *You yell*, "What's the matter with you guys! THIS ISN'T A PIGPEN, IT'S SUPPOSED TO BE A HOME!"

Right way (same scenario): You think, "I'm a walking time bomb waiting to go off. Kids are kids, and we'll worry about picking up at 8 o'clock, like we usually do." *You say*, "Hi guys. I've had a terrible day and need a little space for a few minutes."

Guilt: The poor kid!

Wrong way: It's 2:30 p.m. on a long, boring summer day. Your nine-year-old son asks you to buy him the new, all-the-rage video game. It's not that expensive. You reply, "Not today." He whimpers, "I never get to do anything. This summer really sucks!" *You think*, "I never liked the way my parents treated me. Poor kid. Why am I being so selfish?" *You say*, "All right, but that's all we're getting. I have work to do!"

Right way (same scenario): You think, "His whimpering is testing tactic #4, martyrdom. My boy needs to develop some more constructive ways of entertaining himself." *You say nothing.*

Sadness: Poor me.

Wrong way: Two weeks ago your best friend of fourteen years moved from down the block to a city 900 miles away. It's 9:15 p.m. which is usually story time for your eight-year-old daughter and part of her Basic

Bedtime routine. But over the last couple of weeks you've skipped story time on three occasions and had her go to sleep by herself. You hear, "Mom, are you coming up?" *You think*, "What's the use? I'm tired. She can get herself to sleep." *You say*, "Not tonight, honey."

Right way (same scenario): You think, "I've been sloppy lately with her bedtime. Maintaining the routine and our time together is important. I'll also feel better reading to her than I will sitting down here moping." *You say*, "I'll be up in a second."

Parenting: long hours, no pay, excellent benefits.

Recovering from a Slip-Up

What do you do when you find yourself—over the short or long term—falling back into your old ways? First of all, *accept slipping* as normal. Nobody's perfect, including you, and you shouldn't expect yourself to be. Life—especially with kids—is also quite a bit more complex, messy and challenging than any of us ever anticipated.

Second, it's *back to basics*. Most often, when parents come to me and say "The 1-2-3 is not working anymore," what is happening is a violation of the No-Talking and No-Emotion Rules. The next most common setback is forgetting parenting job #3, relationship strengthening. So we sit down and review *1-2-3 Magic* carefully, and then send Mom and Dad on their way. This brief refresher course usually takes care of the problem.

The fact that you've used *1-2-3 Magic* once and got tripped up a little does not hurt the program's effectiveness the second time around. Turn that 1-2-3 switch back to "On."

When you have caught yourself backsliding say something like this to your kids: "Guys, I'm not doing my job right. You got me frustrated and I'm talking and yelling too much. We're going back to counting." When you've regressed over a longer period, consider redoing the Kickoff Conversation.

Over the course of your kids' growing-up time at your house, you may go through a number of slip ups and recoveries—daily, monthly or even annually. Each time you catch yourself getting careless, just pick yourself up, take a deep breath and go back to what you know works best.

25
Your New Life

It's a brand new life when you enjoy your own kids.

What can you expect from *1-2-3 Magic*? You can expect a more peaceful household, a lot less arguing and fewer angry moments. You can expect to have more fun, and affection will come more easily. The self-esteem of your children will improve and so will yours. You will feel more in control and you will know you are handling things correctly.

What it all boils down to is this: How do you want to spend your time with your kids? One option is that you can spend your time like this:

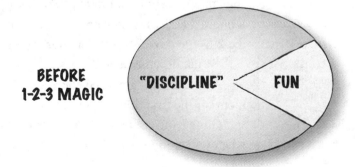

BEFORE
1-2-3 MAGIC

"DISCIPLINE"   FUN

Here the kids are driving you crazy most of the time. You are caught up in frequent but futile attempts at "discipline." There is little time to enjoy the children, educate them or even like them.

On the other hand, you can put some real thought and effort into *1-2-3 Magic* and spend your time like this:

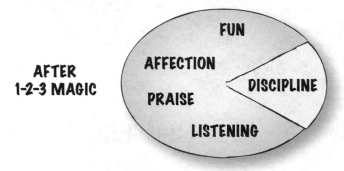

In this situation the proper parenting and family perspective has been established. Sanity is restored by the 1-2-3, making discipline crisp, gentle and efficient. There's less arguing and yelling, and in this more peaceful atmosphere there are more good times. Everyone's self-esteem benefits.

I'll never forget one single mother's comment to me years ago. When she first came into my office, her three kids were driving her nuts. We got her going on *1-2-3 Magic*, and she shaped things up at home very well. One early January day, I saw her for a follow-up visit. She told me Christmas vacation—with all the kids home—had actually gone quite well. She was pleasantly surprised.

Then she said something I've never forgotten: "You know what, though? I never realized how far I'd come until the kids went back to school after vacation."

"What do you mean?" I asked.

A little teary, she paused, then said, "I missed them for the first time in my life."

Quite a turnaround. It's a whole new world when you enjoy your own children.

Good Luck! Don't spend any more days caught up in useless irritation. Take charge of your home today—and start having some fun with your kids!

Appendix:
Further Readings and Resources

Emotional Intelligence

- *Building Moral Intelligence: The Seven Essential Virtues That Teach Kids to Do the Right Thing.* Michele Borba, Ed.D. Jossey-Bass, 2002.

- *Emotional Intelligence: Why It Can Matter More than IQ.* Daniel Goleman, Bantam Books, 1995.

Active Listening and Problem Solving

- *Between Parent and Child.* Haim Ginott. Revised and Updated by Dr. Alice Ginott and Dr. H. Wallace Goddard. Three Rivers Press, 2003.

- *How to Talk So Kids Will Listen and Listen So Kids Will Talk.* Adele Faber and Elaine Mazlish. HarperCollins, 2004.

- *I Can Problem Solve: An Interpersonal Cognitive Problem-Solving Program.* Myrna B. Shure. Research Press, 2001.

Childhood Emotional Problems

- *The Emotional Problems of Normal Children: How Parents Can Understand and Help.* Stanley Turecki, M.D. with Sarah Warnick, Ph.D. Bantam Books, 1994.

- *Freeing Your Child from Anxiety: Powerful, Practical Solutions to Overcome Your Child's Fears, Worries, and Phobias.* Tamar E. Chansky. Broadway, 2004.

Separation and Divorce

- *The Unexpected Legacy of Divorce.* Judith Wallerstein, Julia M. Lewis and Sandra Blakeslee. Hyperion, 2000.

- *Co-Parenting After Divorce: How to Raise Happy, Healthy Children in Two-Home Families.* Winspeed Press, 2000.

Tech and Media

- www.wiredsafety.com *(Internet safety site)*

- www.netsmartz.org *(Very popular safety site used by educators, law enforcement and parents)*

- www.internetsafety.com *(Safe Eyes Internet filter)*

- www.commonsensemedia.org *(One-stop shop for reviews on TV, movies, music, games, books and websites – excellent resource)*

- www.webwatcherkids.com *(Information on monitoring software)*

Parenting Styles

• *Playful Parenting.* Lawrence J. Cohen, Ph.D. Ballantine, 2002.

• *The Power of Loving Discipline.* Karen Miles. Penguin, 2006.

• *The Anger Habit in Parenting.* Carl Semmelroth, Ph.D. Sourcebooks, Inc. 2005.

Child Temperament

• *Understanding Your Child's Temperament.* William B. Carey, M.D. Xlibris Corporation, 2004.

• *Temperament Tools: Working with Your Child's Inborn Traits*, Helen Neville and Diane Clark Johnson. Parenting Press, 1997.

Other Discipline Alternatives

• *Setting Limits with Your Strong-Willed Child: Eliminating Conflict by Establishing Clear, Firm, and Respectful Boundaries.* Robert J. MacKenzie. Three Rivers Press, 2001.

• *Have a New Kid by Friday! How to Change Your Child's Attitude, Behavior & Character in 5 Days.* Kevin Leman. Revell, 2008.

Research on *1-2-3 Magic*

• *Brief Psychoeducational Parenting Program: An Evaluation and 1-Year Followup.* Susan Bradley et al. Journal of the American Academy of Child and Adolescent Psychiatry, 42:10, October, 2003.

• *Authoritative Guide to Self-Help Resources in Mental Health.* John C. Norcross et al. Guilford Press, New York, 2003, pages 136, 139

• *Self-administered psychosocial treatments for children and families.* Frank J. Elgar, Patrick J. McGrath. Journal of Clinical Psychology, Vol. 59 (3), 321-339, 2003

• *Enhancing behavioral and social skill functioning in children newly diagnosed with Attention Deficit/Hyperactivity Disorder in a pediatric setting.* Steve Tutty, M.A., et al. Developmental and Behavioral Pediatrics, Vol.24, No.1, February, 2003.

• *Successful Methods for Increasing and Improving Parent and Child Interactions.* Jane Drapeaux. Paper Presented at the National Head Start Association 24th Annual Training Conference, May 25-31, 1997, Boston, Massachusetts.

• *1-2-3 Magic Part I: Its effectiveness on parental function in child discipline with preschool children.* Yeganeh Salehpour. Dissertation Abstracts International Section A: Humanities & Social Sciences. 57 (3-A), Sept 1996.

Index

1-2-3 Magic Stories and Comments

Excellent parenting book!

I was browsing the book section of my local book store when I happened upon a copy of *1-2-3 Magic* by Thomas Phelan, Ph.D. As the parent of two hyperactive boys, this book was the ONLY book that I have found that is logical and practical in it's parenting applications. This is the best book I've found for effective parenting for those of us blessed with "special" children. I bought two copies (one for myself and one to loan out) The copy I loan out has been across the United States two times in the period of a year. The book was such a success that the school principal ordered a few copies for our school library.

Pediatrician: Every parent should read this book!

This book describes an easy, effective method that any caretaker can use to maintain control of their household without resorting to violence. Most importantly, it instructs caretakers on the appropriate use of time-out and demonstrates how effective it can be when used properly. As a pediatrician, I believe all caretakers should read it and cannot recommend it highly enough.

It really works!

Our three-year-old's pre-school teacher recommended this book to us. We were skeptical in the beginning to say the least. After reading the book we were still a bit skeptical. How could this simple method of counting to three work? Yet we tried the 1-2-3 method and after about five days our daughter understood what we meant and is now a success story of "*1-2-3 Magic*"!

The Best Parenting book I've read.

This book was referred to me by a therapist as a tool to use for my five-year-old son who was exceedingly frustrated and prone to "meltdowns." The methods espoused by Dr. Phelan are so simple and yet so completely effective! They are also very humane. I highly recommend this book to every parent who wants to restore peace in the home.

This is a 5+!

This book as changed our lives. The impact of silence is the most powerful parenting tool I have ever encountered. I am the mom of 3 very active boys who used to rule the roost. Now I am calling all the shots and we are the most functional family you could ever imagine. I would love to thank the authors of this book for saving our sanity and our lives. I have been your best advertisement for your book. Everyone I know is reading it with the same amazing results. Wish I would of had this from day one. Oh well, everything falls into place on its own... Thank you again.

I wish I had read this book months ago!

We had tried everything to try and show our 3-year-old son who is in charge. We couldn't go to restaurants (or almost any public place for that matter) without it ending in a meltdown and being bitten, pinched and hit by our son. Even at home if he didn't get his way he would bite/hit/pinch/scream. We agreed not to spank, but found ourselves yelling often. Many days I ended up in tears. My son's preschool teacher recommended this book. I stayed up almost all night one night reading it, and put it into action. It has changed everything! Not only does the counting method really work (I had sort of used my own counting before, but I wasn't following the "no talking, no emotions" rule), but we just feel more in charge and in control, which our son seems to sense and respond to. He is much better behaved all the way around, but if he does have a meltdown it is gone right after "that's two." I can't believe what a difference this has made in my house!

Professional Educator: Wonderful behavior plan for all children.

I have found the book to be instrumental in my profession—education. When Dr. Phelan's methods are used correctly, tremendous improvements are seen quickly. I recommended the book to all parents of young children, educators, and behavior specialists.

So simple it works!

Its just amazing! At your wits end buy this book!

You have to get this book!

This book is very easy to understand and to follow. I bought the book and my husband and I read it in less than one day. By that night, we had a family meeting to discuss. The one thing that makes this book different from any other discipline books is that it is a very easy process and gives you examples of EVERY possible scenario you could encounter (in the car, in the store, what if they say no, what if they talk back, etc.) It's got all the answers. It made me a believer when my 7- and 9-year-old boys were fighting in the car and all I had to do was say "That's 1 for both of you," and for the first time EVER there wasn't another word out of either of them. My husband and I couldn't stop giggling we were so excited!! We kept looking at them to make sure they weren't fighting in quiet because we couldn't believe it. But they weren't! The fight had actually stopped. You HAVE to get this book!

No PsychoBabble.

You don't need to "understand" your "difficult" or "regular" child to make this method work. This book shows you (not the kids) how to be in charge and get peace into your everyday life with a VERY simple method. Yes, you can control big, bad behaviors as well as those little annoying behaviors: arguing, badgering, whining, complaining, etc. A second method is presented (which also works) for getting kids to go to bed at night. We have had great success for 2 years now with ages 3 to 7.

1-2-3 Magic.

This book makes a difference that you would never imagine possible. Within 48 hours my 5- and 7-year-old were different children. It is presented in a humorous yet truthful and scientific way. When you sit back and think about it, kids are not born with manners and respect. They have to learn it in a way that their psychological ages are able to process and learn. We lose sight of their comprehension ability. If you find your-self repeating the same lines over and over in frustration, read this book and change your household! Loved it!

Life-saving book!

This book changed my life as the mom of a very strong-willed daughter. I bought this book when she was three and was disturbing the peace for our whole family. Within two days I saw a VERY big improvement in her behavior and our friends even said she seemed happier, knowing what the rules were. Three years later we still use the methods in this book, though she doesn't need it much any more. I mostly use these tips on her younger sister who's inherited the role of problem child in the family. Great book!

Who rules YOUR house? YOU or your KIDS?

READ THIS BOOK if you want YOUR rights as a PARENT reinstated. It needs to be passed out in the maternity ward as far as I'm concerned.

Simple, effective, painless.

Dr. Phelan's book is not just about a theory. It is about a system that work—like "magic"! In a humorous, easy-to-read format, Dr. Phelan describes a simple, non-harming method for stopping misbehavior and starting desired behaviors, based on basic behavioral principles and child development. But what if ...? The author has an amazing ability to supply the reader with the answers to all of the "what ifs" and "yeah, buts."

I feel like I finally found "The Manual."

I love this book for its direct step-by-step approach. The author seems to have thought of every contingency and provides a method to handle it. This method really does work.

If your kids out of control, try this. It really works!

I worked in a psych hospital for a couple of years with highly assaultive, out of control children and teenagers. This method worked for us, and some of the teens I worked with should have been in jail, to tell the truth. This method sounds too good to be true, but believe me, if you're consistent with it, and do it as described, it WILL work for you.